Liven Up Your Library

CREATIVE & INEXPENSIVE PROMGRAMMING IDEAS

Jennifer A. Wetzel

UpstartBooks™

Madison, Wisconsin

This book is dedicated to the staff and students at Hendron-Lone Oak Elementary School who provided the inspiration for these materials, and to my parents who always encouraged my dreams.
—J. A. W.

Published by UpstartBooks
4810 Forest Run Road
Madison, WI 53704
1-800-448-4887

© Jennifer A. Wetzel, 2009
Cover design: Debra Neu

The paper used in this publication meets the minimum requirements of American National Standard for Information Science — Permanence of Paper for Printed Library Material. ANSI/NISO Z39.48-1992.

Table of Contents

Introduction

Goals

While compiling the units and accompanying materials found in this book, I had several goals. First, I wanted to teach library and information skills in a fun but purposeful manner. How many of us have inwardly groaned at the thought of trying to explain the Dewey Decimal system to small children? It's a daunting task, but one that can be done. Throughout my teaching experience, I have found that the enthusiasm and creativity I demonstrated led to an increased enthusiasm from the students. So, if we want the library to be fun, we must first be fun-loving!

Second, I wanted my library media center to be accessible to all students and for lessons to reach even the most challenged learners. I felt that when teaching students skills for using the library and for accessing information, I must view it from their perspective and break the material down in a manner understandable to them. As a result, I began developing lessons and units that utilized the students' personal interests to reinforce information literacy skills.

Third, I wanted to create purposeful lessons in my library media center. I believe in standards-based units of study and starting with the end in mind. While planning, I first ask, "What do I want my students to gain from this instruction?" After determining what I want them to have learned by the end of the unit, I work backward to plan lesson activities that will lead to the independent work in the culminating activity. In this way, I feel that I can better teach the students in an effective, purposeful manner. I hope that you can adapt these lessons to your own situation and students. Most importantly, I hope that you have as much fun as I do!

Standards

The units in this book are aligned with the American Association of School Librarians' *Standards for the 21st Century Learner*. These standards focus on students' ability to acquire and utilize information, share knowledge, and pursue personal interests. As a model for information literacy skills, the *Standards for the 21st Century Learner* also promote ethical behavior and equitable access to information for all students. A detailed list of the standards is available from the American Association of School Librarians. Information for acquiring the standards is located in the resource chapter.

Chapter Format

The chapters in this book are organized according to topic and include the targeted grade levels for each. Each lesson is designed to be completed in one 30-minute class period unless it is otherwise noted. Chapters utilize the following format:

Lessons

Lesson Overview

Materials

A list of all items needed to effectively implement the lesson activities.

Preparation

A list of items to prepare before the lesson or steps for gathering needed items before implementing the lesson.

Standards

A list of the *Standards for the 21st Century Learner* addressed in the lesson.

Lesson Objectives

The goals for student learning and the desired student behavior that demonstrates mastery of lesson.

Lesson Plan

Steps for implementing the lesson with students.

Rubric

Tools for assessing the culminating activity. See page 159 for more information about creating rubrics.

Extension Idea

Ideas for extending the lesson beyond the unit to further engage students in the learning process or to allow for independent learning.

Reproducibles

Worksheets, posters, bookmarks, and other materials needed for implementing the lessons within each chapter.

Games Format

The chapter on review games utilizes the following format instead of the lesson plan format:

Standards

A list of the *Standards for the 21st Century Learner* addressed while playing the review game.

Objectives

The goals for student learning while engaged in the review game.

Materials

A list of all materials needed to prepare the game and implement it.

Preparation

Steps needed to prepare the game for play with students.

Explanation

Steps for playing the game and engaging students in review.

Resources

The book concludes with a resource chapter that includes bibliographic and purchasing information for the books and materials found in each unit. It also includes the URLs for Web sites mentioned and utilized throughout the book.

Classroom Management

Effective classroom management is essential for implementing lessons and teaching information literacy skills. It allows students to learn and acquire new skills in a setting that is equitable to everyone's learning needs. For this reason, I have included five classroom management techniques that I have found effective within my own library media center.

Wristbands

No time to reward every student? Does a back-to-back fixed schedule prevent you from discussing student behavior with teachers? Use this cheap and fast reward to let everyone know which students did a great job in the library! Photocopy the wristbands on pages 9–10 onto colored paper and then cut apart. Keep a stack handy in the library. As students perform especially well or leave for the day, tape or staple a wristband around their arm. Teachers will be able to see in an instant which students were outstanding!

Magic Wand

Give students a taste of magic to help them behave! To help my students stay on task, I use a star-shaped musical chime from Tree Blocks (see purchasing information on page 154) to alert them to who has the desired behavior and who does not. By holding the wand in a certain way while tapping the students' heads gently, I can produce a ringing sound. I can also tap the wand without making the ringing sound. I tell my students that the wand is "magic" and tells me exactly who is behaving. Students beg to be "tapped" to see how they are behaving and even love to see their teachers get tapped too!

Brain Bubbles

For brain bubbles, I cover a bottle of bubble blow liquid with a slip of paper that says "Brain Bubbles." From the first day of the school year, it sits displayed on a shelf and students become very curious about it. When we play review games or take tests, I blow the "Brain Bubbles," explaining to students that each bubble contains the answers they need for the day. I allow each student to catch a brain bubble, giving them an added boost of confidence.

Build-a-Bookworm

Before the beginning of a new school year, buy a chart and laminate it. This will be your Build-a-Bookworm chart. Using a dry erase marker, list each homeroom class vertically on the chart. Post this chart outside of the library door. Determine how many "bookworm" sections classes will earn at each level of the rubric. At the beginning of the year, explain the contest to the students. Each nine weeks, there will be a contest to see which class is the most well behaved while visiting the library. At the end of each library visit, students will be evaluated according to their behavior. Then, they will add the appropriate number of sections onto their bookworm. Bonus sections can be earned by going above and beyond the expected behaviors. At the end of the nine weeks, the library media specialist will count to see which class earned the largest number of sections for their bookworm. That class earns special recognition with a sign that hangs outside of the library and wins a party during their next library visit. At the party, provide drinks, snacks, and a small prize for each member of the class. At the beginning of the next nine weeks, the slate is wiped clean and each class starts building their bookworm again.

Miss Lotta Scales Doll

Read *The Library Dragon* by Carmen Agra Deedy and then use the corresponding doll (see purchasing information on page 154) to help students monitor their behavior in the library. The doll can be flipped from Miss Lotty to Miss Lotta Scales, the "library dragon," when students are not following rules. Or, just pull the tail out on the Miss Lotty side as a warning. This works very well when you choose one student to monitor the behavior and do the flipping. I've learned that they're harder on themselves than I would ever be!

Red Hot Reader Wristbands

I'm a Red Hot Reader

I'm a Red Hot Reader

I'm a Red Hot Reader

I'm a Red Hot Reader

I'm a Red Hot Reader

I'm a Red Hot Reader

I'm a Red Hot Reader

I'm a Red Hot Reader

I'm a Red Hot Reader

Performance Wristbands

_____ **was a great reader today!**

_____ **was a good helper in the library!**

_____ **took good care of a library book!**

_____ **returned their library book on time!**

_____ **knows how to put books away!**

_____ **is a good friend!**

_____ **was a great student today!**

Thanks to _____ for being a good leader!

I´m a proud of _____ !

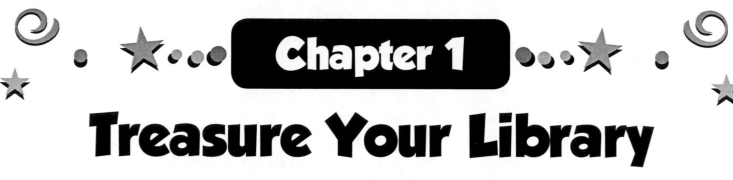

Treasure Your Library

> **Overview**
>
> Welcome students back to school with this action-packed orientation unit. Through games such as "Library Survivor" and a card catalog treasure hunt, students will keep the spirit of summer alive as they reconnect with all the riches that the library has to offer.
>
> **Grade Level: 3–5**
>
> **Chapter Materials**
>
> The following materials will be needed for each lesson in the chapter:
>
> - Library media center rules poster (see page 16)
> - Laminating machine
> - Palm trees and other tropical decorations
> - Hula skirt ensemble or Hawaiian shirt and shorts, flip-flops
> - "Treasure" (prizes) for game winners, such as bookmarks, candy, etc.
> - Treasure chest (this can be made by wrapping a large shoe box in gold wrapping paper)
>
> **Chapter Preparation**
>
> 1. Copy and laminate the library media center rules poster.
> 2. Decorate the reading area with palm trees and other tropical décor.
> 3. Create your treasure chest and fill it with prizes.
> 4. Dress the part before each lesson: a hula skirt ensemble or Hawaiian shirt and shorts with flip-flops.

Lesson 1: Library Survivor

Time Required: 1–2 class periods

Standards

1.1.2 Use prior and background knowledge as context for new learning.

1.1.6 Read, view, and listen for information presented in any format (e.g., textual, visual, media, digital) in order to make inferences and gather meaning.

Lesson Objectives

1. Students will correctly identify rules and responsibilities of the library media center.
2. Students will demonstrate correct behaviors to use in the library media center.

Additional Materials

- Survivor Voting Sheet (page 17)
- Pencils

Lesson Preparation

- Copy the Survivor Voting Sheet (one per student).

Lesson Plan

1. When students arrive at class, explain that the reading area is decorated for a special reason. Explain that even though school is starting again, you still want to be on vacation. So, you decided to bring the beach back to school with you!

2. Tell students that for the next several class periods, they will be visiting the beach with you each time the class visits the library. You think that there is as much treasure in the library as there is on a beach or in the ocean. So, to get back into the mindset for school, it is time to "treasure your library"!

3. Use the poster of library media center rules to review expected behavior for the library media center.

4. Tell students that today, everyone will play "Library Survivor" through an improvisation activity.

5. Divide the class into small groups and assign a library media center rule to each group.

6. Tell students that they will plan a small skit that shows someone breaking the rule they have been assigned. They will have a short amount of time in class to practice their skit. Then, each group will perform its skit for the class. The class will then vote groups off the "island" and select a "Library Survivor."

7. Give groups time to plan and rehearse their skits.

8. Have each group perform a skit for the class.

9. Give each student a Survivor Voting Sheet (page 17). Have students vote for a group to "kick off the island" because it did not effectively present its assigned rule. Then, have students vote for the "Library Survivors," or the group that was the most effective and creative in representing its library media center rule.

10. Tally the results. Announce in random order the groups that are being "kicked off the island." Then, announce the winning group and allow its members to select a prize from the treasure chest.

Lesson 2: X Marks the Spot

Time Required: 1 class period

Standards

1.1.2 Use prior and background knowledge as context for new learning.

1.1.6 Read, view, and listen for information presented in any format (e.g., textual, visual, media, digital) in order to make inferences and gather meaning.

4.2.3 Demonstrate teamwork by working productively with others.

Lesson Objectives

1. Students will correctly identify areas and resources available in the library media center.

2. Students will work collaboratively in small groups to communicate learned information during group discussion.

Additional Materials

- Library Media Map (see lesson preparation and then example on page 18)

- Stickers, several different styles

Lesson Preparation

1. Create a simple map of your library media center (see example on page 18). On the map, mark an "X" in each area that you wish students to visit, and create a "You Are Here" arrow to help orient them.

2. Make one copy of the map for each small group of 3–4 students.

3. Place a sheet of stickers in each area of the library media center that you have marked with an "X" on the map. Put the stickers in spots where students will have to search a bit to find them. Each area should have a different style of sticker.

Lesson Plan

1. Remind students that there is as much treasure in the library as there is on a beach or in the ocean. Today, they will find out where they can locate some of the treasure available in the library media center.

2. Ask students how pirates and other people find buried treasure. Wait for their responses. Affirm that, yes, pirates do find treasure with treasure maps. That's why many people say "X Marks the Spot."

3. Explain that in the library, there is also lots of treasure to find! Today, they will be using maps of the library to find where the treasured reading materials are located.

4. Divide the class into groups of 3–4 students and give each group a map. Explain that their job is to use the map to locate each of the spots marked with an "X." Once they find the spot, they must write which section of the library it is on the map. They must also locate the sheet of stickers hidden in that section, place a sticker over the X on the map, and then return the sticker sheet to its hiding place. The first team to return a correctly completed map wins a prize.

5. Give students time to locate sections marked on the map. Continue play until all teams have completed the map.

6. Gather students in the reading area of the library media center.

7. Announce the winners of the game and allow them to select a prize from the treasure chest.

8. Review the map with students. Ask them to name each marked section of the map. As they name the sections, also ask them to review what types of "treasure" or resources are found in that area. For instance, students should identify that the fiction section contains make-believe stories.

Lesson 3: The Card Catalog: Riddled with Treasure !

Time Required: 2 class periods

Standards

1.1.2 Use prior and background knowledge as context for new learning.

1.1.6 Read, view, and listen for information presented in any format (e.g., textual, visual, media, digital) in order to make inferences and gather meaning.

4.2.4 Demonstrate teamwork by working productively with others.

Lesson Objectives

1. Students will correctly utilize the card catalog to locate resources in the library media center.

2. Students will work collaboratively in small groups to communicate learned information during group discussion.

Additional Materials

- Riddled With Treasure! worksheets on pages 19–20. Select the scrambled (page 20) or unscrambled (page 19) version to give to give your students (scrambled is more challenging). IMPORTANT: be sure to review the answer key on page 21 to ensure that you have the mystery titles from the worksheets in your collection. If you do not, create customized questions based on your library's collection, and print them on the Riddled With Treasure! worksheet template on page 22.

- Computer with automated card catalog

- LCD projector

Lesson Preparation

1. Copy the Riddled With Treasure! worksheet (one per small group).

2. Connect the LCD projector to the computer.

Lesson Plan

1. Review with students that you are still bringing summer vacation to school with the

"Treasure Your Library" theme. Today, they will discover how to find out whether if the library media center has a specific resource and where it is located.

2. Turn on the LCD projector and ensure that all students are sitting where they can see the screen.

3. Using the projector, demonstrate how to access the automated card catalog. Then, demonstrate how to locate books using the author, title, subject, series, and keyword searches.

4. Divide students into small groups. Give each group a Riddled With Treasure! worksheet. Explain that they will work in their groups to fill in the blanks using their library knowledge and the automated card catalog. If they locate the correct answers, then the circled letters will form the answer to the riddle on the worksheet. The first team to locate the correct answers and solve the riddle will win prizes. **(Answer: "pie rats ahoy")**

5. Give students time to complete the worksheet. Continue play until all teams have completed the worksheet.

6. Gather students in the reading area of the library media center.

7. Announce the winners of the game and allow them to select a prize from the treasure chest.

8. Review answers with the students and remind them of the various ways to search the automated card catalog.

Lesson 4: Digging for Treasure Call Number Review

Standards

1.1.2   Use prior and background knowledge as context for new learning.

1.1.4   Find, evaluate, and select appropriate sources to answer questions.

4.2.5   Demonstrate teamwork by working productively with others.

Lesson Objectives

1. Students will correctly identify call numbers to locate resources within the library media center.

2. Students will work collaboratively in small groups to locate resources within the library media center.

Additional Materials

*   Digging for Treasure Template on page 23
*   Gold Coin templates on page 24
*   Yellow copy paper
*   Shelf markers (one per group)
*   Marker

Lesson Preparation

1. Make several copies of the Digging for Treasure template. On the templates, record the title and call numbers of books currently available and checked in at your library media center. Cut slips apart.

2. Copy Gold Coin Templates on yellow copy paper and cut apart.

3. Make up team names, such as the Book Buccaneers or Poetry Pirates, and write each team name on a shelf marker.

Lesson Plan

1. Remind students that there is as much treasure in the library as there is on a beach or in the ocean. Today, they will review call numbers so that they can independently locate resources in the library media center.

2. Review how fiction, easy, nonfiction, and biography books are shelved. Also review other special collections in the library media center that you would like students to be able to utilize.

3. Explain to students that today, they are going on a treasure hunt to locate specific resources within the library media center. They now know where different sections are located within the library media center and how to use the card catalog to locate what resources are available. Today, they will practice locating resources on the shelf by using call numbers.

4. Divide the students into teams and assign each team a name and shelf marker. Then, give each team a slip of paper with the title of a book and its call number. As a team, they must work together to locate that book on the shelf. Then, they must put their team shelf marker in its place and bring the book with the slip of paper to you for checking. If they have found the correct book, they will be given a gold coin. Then, they will return the book to the spot where they found it and remove their shelf marker. After completing that step, they will be given another slip of paper to continue to earn gold coins for their team. At the end of class, the team with the most gold coins will win a prize. If there is a tie between teams, then the team with the best cooperation will be declared the winners.

5. Give each team a slip of paper with a call number and title. Once all teams have their first slip of paper, play begins.

6. Continue the review as time allows.

7. When five minutes remain, call time. Have students return materials to shelves, gather shelf markers, and straighten the library media center.

8. Announce the winners of the game and allow them to select a prize from the treasure chest.

Treasure Hunt Rubric

CATEGORY	4	3	2	1
Cooperation	Always listens to and supports the efforts of others.	Usually listens to and supports the efforts of others.	Often listens to and supports the efforts of others, but does not always cooperate as a team.	Rarely listens to and supports the efforts of others. Often does not work cooperatively.
Focus	Consistently stays focused on the task.	Focuses on the task and what needs to be done most of the time.	Focuses on the task and what needs to be done some of the time.	Rarely focuses on the task and what needs to be done.
Call Number	Always recognizes and understands how to use a call number to locate a resource.	Usually recognizes and understands how to use a call number to locate a resource.	Sometimes recognizes and understands how to use a call number to locate a resource.	Rarely or never recognizes and understands how to use a call number to locate a resource.
Shelving	Always returns materials to correct space on shelf.	Usually returns materials to correct space on shelf.	Sometimes returns materials to correct space on shelf.	Rarely or never returns materials to correct space on shelf.

Extension Idea

Provide each student with the Treasure Your Library book review template on page 25. Have students write a review of their favorite book. Use the reviews to decorate a bulletin board with the theme, "Treasure Your Library: Read these Gems!"

Library Media Center Rules

- Follow directions.

- Always come prepared.

- Be respectful of others.

- Keep noise at the appropriate level for the activity.

- Accept the consequences of your actions.

- Try new things.

Survivor Voting Sheet

Name of group to vote off the island

Name of group to stay on the island

Library Media Map

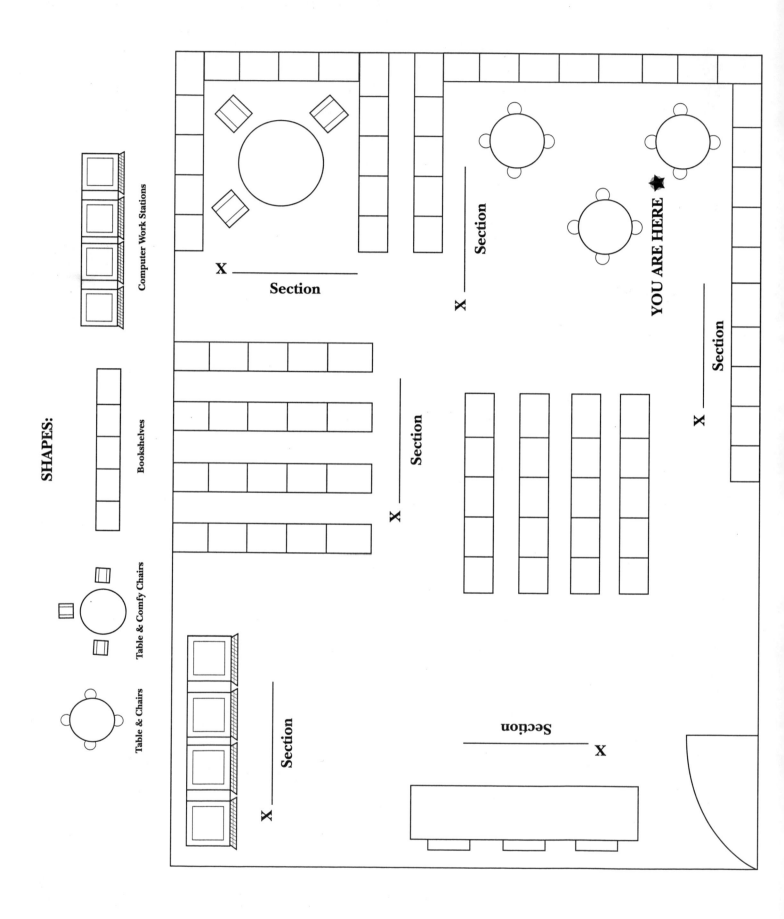

Riddled With Treasure!

X marks the spot! Use the card catalog to walk your way through the treasure map! Each clue will help you find the answers in the card catalog. After you fill in the answers, the circled letters will solve the riddle below. The first team to find the correct answers and solve the riddle visits the treasure chest!

1. *Hatchet* is a famous book about wilderness survival written by _ _ _ _ _
    Ⓞ_ _ _ _ _ _.

2. Books that contain factual information are shelved in the _ _ _ _ _ _ _Ⓞ_ _ section of the library.

3. Author Kate DiCamillo wrote a book about a toy rabbit. It's called *The Miraculous Journey of* Ⓞ_ _ _ Ⓞ_ _ _ _ _ _ _ _.

4. Robert Munsch wrote a book about being a copycat called _ _ _ _ _ Ⓞ_ _ _ '_ _ _ _ _Ⓞ_ _ _.

5. *Chrysanthemum* was written by author _ _ _ _ _ _ _ _ _ _ _Ⓞ.

6. The *Magic Tree House* series was written _ Ⓞ_ _ _ _ _ _ _ _ _ _.

7. Books such as the dictionary, encyclopedia and _Ⓞ_ _ _ _ _ _ _ _ can be found in the reference section of the library.

8. If I did a keyword search for "Abraham Lincoln," I would find out that books about his life are shelved in the _ _Ⓞ_ _ _ _ _Ⓞ section.

Riddle

What did the captain say when he discovered someone stealing his desserts?

_ _ _ _ _ _ _ _ _ _ _ _ _ _!

Riddled With Treasure!

X marks the spot! Use card catalog to walk your way through the treasure map!
Each clue will help you find the answers in the card catalog. After you fill in the answers,
unscramble the circled letters to solve the riddle below. The first team to find the correct
answers and solve the riddle visits the treasure chest!

1. Author Kate DiCamillo wrote a book about a toy rabbit. It's called *The Miraculous Journey of* ◯ _ _ _ ◯ _ _ _ _ _ _ _ _ .

2. The *Magic Tree House* series was written by _ ◯ _ _ _ _ _ _ _ _ _ _ .

3. *Hatchet* is a famous book about wilderness survival written by _ _ _ _ ◯ _ _ _ _ _ _ .

4. If I did a keyword search for "Abraham Lincoln," I would find out that books about his life are shelved in the _ _ ◯ _ _ _ _ _ ◯ section.

5. *Chrysanthemum* was written by author _ _ _ _ _ _ _ _ _ _ ◯ .

6. Books that contain factual information are shelved in the _ _ _ _ _ _ _ ◯ _ _ section of the library.

7. Robert Munsch wrote a book about being a copycat called _ _ _ _ _ _ ◯ _ _ _ ' _ _ _ _ _ ◯ _ _ _ .

8. Books such as the dictionary, encyclopedia and _ ◯ _ _ _ _ _ _ _ _ can be found in the reference section of the library.

Riddle

What did the captain say when he discovered someone stealing his desserts?

_ _ _ _ _ _ _ _ _ _ _ _ _ _ !

Riddled With Treasure! Answer Key

X marks the spot! Use card catalog to walk your way through the treasure map!
Each clue will help you find the answers in the card catalog. After you fill in the answers, the circled letters will solve the riddle below. The first team to find the correct answers and solve the riddle visits the treasure chest!

1. *Hatchet* is a famous book about wilderness survival written by G A R Y (P) A U L S E N.

2. Books that contain factual information are shelved in the N O N F I C T (I) O N section of the library.

3. Author Kate DiCamillo wrote a book about a toy rabbit. It's called *The Miraculous Journey of* (E) D W A (R) D   T U L A N E.

4. Robert Munsch wrote a book about being a copycat called S T E P H (A) N I E 'S P O N Y (T) A I L.

5. *Chrysanthemum* was written by author K E V I N   H E N K E (S).

6. The *Magic Tree House* series was written by M (A) R Y   O S B O R N E.

7. Books such as the dictionary, encyclopedia and T (H) E S A U R U S can be found in the reference section of the library.

8. If I did a keyword search for "Abraham Lincoln," I would find out that books about his life are shelved in the B I (O) G R A P H (Y) section.

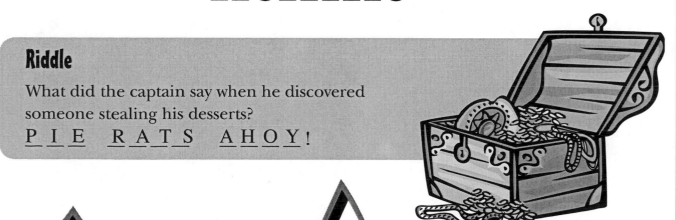

Riddle

What did the captain say when he discovered someone stealing his desserts?
P I E   R A T S   A H O Y !

Riddled With Treasure!

X marks the spot! Use card catalog to walk your way through the treasure map!
Each clue will help you find the answers in the card catalog. After you fill in the answers, locate one of the books on the shelf. The first team to find the correct answers and one of the books visits the treasure chest!

Digging for Treasure

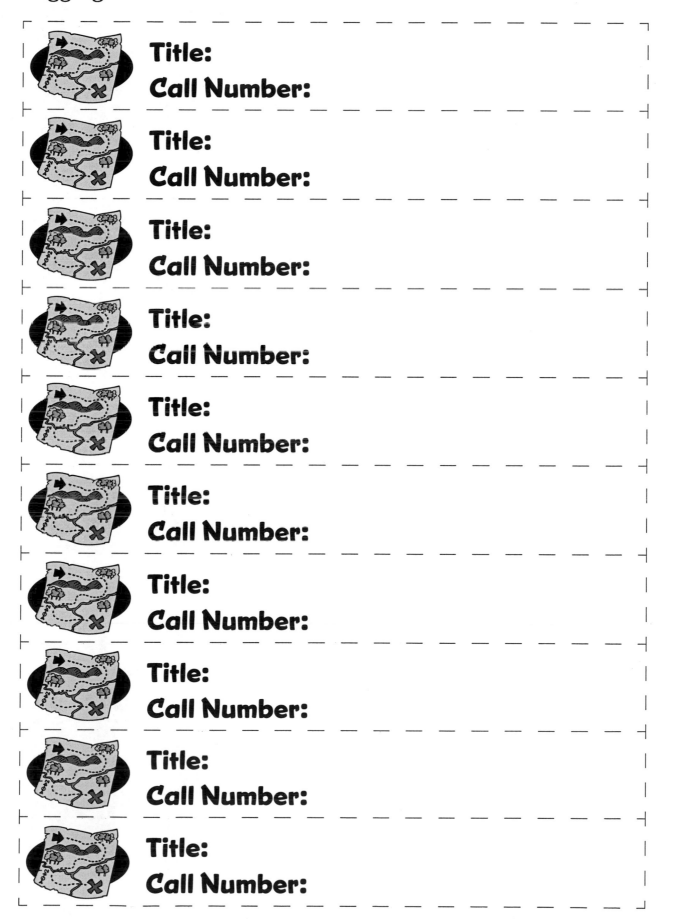

Title:

Call Number:

Title:

Call Number:

Title:

Call Number:

Title:

Call Number:

Title:

Call Number:

Title:

Call Number:

Title:

Call Number:

Title:

Call Number:

Title:

Call Number:

Title:

Call Number:

Gold Coin Template

Treasure Your Library:
A Gem of a Book

Title of book: _____

Author's Name: _____

Call Number: _____

This book is about _____

_____

_____

_____

_____

If you like books that are _____

_____

then you should read this book!

This book is a real "gem" because _____

_____

_____

_____

_____

_____

_____ .

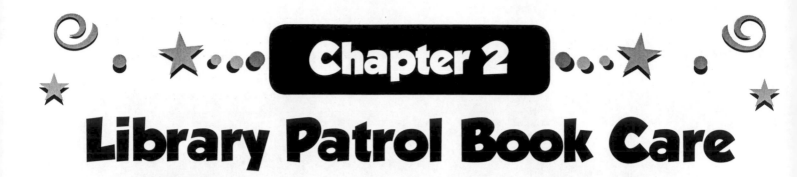

Chapter 2
Library Patrol Book Care

Many students feel empowered when they are entrusted with the care and protection of the library. This chapter offers ideas for encouraging responsible patronage through a sense of guardianship.

Grade Level: K–2

Chapter Materials

The following materials will be needed for each lesson in the chapter:

- Wanted Posters (pages 30—34)
- Sheriff badge (purchase or make by cutting a star out of gold construction paper)
- Laminating machine

Chapter Preparation:

1. Copy and laminate the Wanted Posters.
2. Purchase or make your sheriff badge and pin or tape it to your shirt before each class.

Lesson 1: The Patrol

Time Required: 1 class period

Standards

1.1.2 Use prior and background knowledge as context for new learning.

1.1.6 Read, view, and listen for information presented in any format (e.g., textual, visual, media, digital) in order to make inferences and gather meaning.

Lesson Objectives

1. Students will correctly identify ways to care for the library media center.
2. Students will correctly identify ways to care for library books.
3. Students will demonstrate correct behaviors to use in the library media center.

Additional Materials

- Library Patrol stickers (page 35)
- Sticker paper (such as White Sticker Project Paper from Avery)
- Torn, scribbled, and otherwise damaged books

Chapter Preparation

1. Copy the Library Patrol stickers on the sticker paper and cut apart (one sticker per student.)
2. Set the damaged books aside for use in lesson.
3. Mess up several sections of library shelving by turning books backwards, leaving books on the floor, and placing books askew on the shelves.

Lesson Plan

1. When students arrive to class, explain to them that you are wearing a badge for a special reason. Ask students if they know who usually wears a badge. Give students time to answer.

2. Explain that sheriffs wear badges. You are wearing one because you are the sheriff of the Library Patrol! Tell students that the Library Patrol takes care of the library media center and looks out for library outlaws. After they catch the outlaws, they teach them how to care for books and help them to join the Library Patrol.

3. Explain to students that you need more officers in the Library Patrol because some of the library outlaws have been messing up the books and library media center lately.

4. Ask students to look around the library media center and see if they can spot any problems with the shelving. Call on students to point out the problem areas and ask them to fix them. Review your library's rules for proper library shelving.

5. Pick up the stack of "hurt" books to show students. Hold one book up at a time and dramatically show students the "injuries" that the book suffered from the library outlaws. Review book care rules with students as you show the hurt books.

6. Explain to students that they must be on the lookout for library outlaws. Show students the wanted posters of library outlaws. Hold the posters up one at a time and explain what these people did:

   a. Scribbling Sam colors and writes in books.

   b. Ripping Ryan cuts and rips pages.

   c. Bookworm Brittany likes to chew on books, and even allows her pets and baby siblings to chomp them, as well!

   d. Overdue Olivia does not return books on time.

   e. Abandon Alex leaves books on the bus, in the cafeteria, on the playground, on the floor, and in other inappropriate locations.

7. Explain to students that in order to become library patrol officers, they must learn the patrol laws. Each time they see evidence of a library outlaw, they must report it to the sheriff (you) as soon as possible and fix the damage. They must also keep everyone on alert so the library outlaws can be caught.

8. Congratulate students on becoming Library Patrol officers and give each student a sticker.

Lesson 2: Patrol in Action

Time Required: 1 class period

Standards

1.1.2 Use prior and background knowledge as context for new learning.

1.1.6 Read, view, and listen for information presented in any format (e.g., textual, visual, media, digital) in order to make inferences and gather meaning.

3.1.2 Participate and collaborate as members of a social and intellectual network of learners.

Lesson Objectives

1. Students will correctly identify ways to care for the library media center.

2. Students will correctly utilize shelf markers.

3. Students will correctly utilize bookmarks.

Additional Materials

- Shelf markers
- Bookmarks
- Library Patrol bookmarks (page 36)
- Book with dog-eared pages

Lesson Preparation

- Copy the Library Patrol bookmarks (one per student).

- Hang the Wanted posters above the dry erase board or teaching area.

Lesson Plan

1. Review the information about the library patrol that students learned in Lesson 1, as well as the information about library book care.

2. Explain to students that today, they will learn two additional library patrol laws. Tell students that you have noticed that many students mess up the shelves as they look for books. To truly be library patrol officers, they must learn to use their library tools. One of the library patrol's greatest tools is the shelf marker. When used correctly, the shelf marker can foil the work of library outlaws. Explain that shelf markers are not used for hitting one another, the books, or anything in the library.

3. Tell students that the next library patrol law is the correct use of a shelf marker. Take students to a shelf and demonstrate the correct way to use the shelf marker.

4. Have each student take a shelf marker and line up in front of a section of shelving.

5. Have students practice using the shelf markers until they are able to do it independently.

6. Praise students' efforts on learning a new patrol law and explain that there is one more law to learn. Gather them around you.

7. Hold up the book with dog-eared pages. Tell students that this happens when library outlaws do not use bookmarks. Explain how folding pages down can rip pages and demonstrate the correct way to use bookmarks.

8. Give students a copy of the library patrol bookmark and give them time to color it.

Lesson 3: Help Wanted

Time Required: 1 class period

Standards

1.1.2 Use prior and background knowledge as context for new learning.

1.1.6 Read, view, and listen for information presented in any format (e.g., textual, visual, media, digital) in order to make inferences and gather meaning.

3.1.2 Participate and collaborate as members of a social and intellectual network of learners.

3.1.3 Use writing and speaking skills to communicate new understandings effectively.

3.2.3 Demonstrate teamwork by working productively with others.

Lesson Objectives

1. Students will correctly identify ways to care for library books.

2. Students will work collaboratively in small groups to communicate learned information in poster format.

Additional Materials

• *The Incredible Book Eating Boy* by Oliver Jeffers

• Wanted posters (page 30—34)

• Dry erase board and dry erase marker

• Help Wanted poster template (page 37)

• Posterboard for each group, crayons, colored pencils, or markers

Lesson Preparation

1. Divide class roster into small groups of 3-4.

2. Copy the Help Wanted poster (one per group).

Lesson Plan

1. Review with students the information about the Library Patrol that they learned in Lessons 1 and 2. Point to each poster of the library outlaws and review with students what that outlaw did. Review how those actions do not help the library media center or library books.

2. Show students the cover of the book *The Incredible Book Eating Boy* by Oliver Jeffers. Explain that you think the library outlaws are influencing some of the older students. Read and discuss the story.

3. Explain to students that you need more Library Patrol officers to prevent examples like the one seen in the book. You are proud that they became Library Patrol officers and are working hard to take care of the library. However, the library outlaws are always around, even when their class does not visit the library. As a result, they must

try to recruit students from other classes to become Library Patrol officers. That way, the library media center will be protected at all times.

4. Draw a t-chart on the dry erase board. Label one side "Do" and one side "Don't." Explain to students that a t-chart is used to compare two things. Today, they are going to compare behaviors that help to take care of library books, and behaviors that don't take care of library books.

5. Ask students to name a behavior and under which side of the chart it should be listed. Discuss that behavior with students and how it helps or hurts library books.

6. Continue making a list until students have covered the majority of behaviors discussed in previous lessons.

7. Explain to students that they will work in small groups to create "Help Wanted" posters. These posters will list the characteristics needed in Library Patrol officers and tell other students how to become officers. For example, one group might list "Library Patrol officers take books home in their backpacks" and illustrate a picture of someone placing a book in a backpack.

8. Give each group a Help Wanted poster template and allow them to work together to create their poster.

9. Hang posters throughout school hallways.

Help Wanted Poster Rubric

CATEGORY	4	3	2	1
Cooperation	Worked well together and used time wisely in class.	Worked well together and mostly used time wisely in class.	Worked somewhat well together but did not use time wisely in class.	Did not work well together and did not use time wisely in class.
Illustrations	Illustrations are neat, recognizable, and depict the text.	Illustrations are mainly neat, recognizable, and depict the text.	Illustrations are neat or recognizable, but do not depict the text.	Illustrations are not neat or recognizable, and do not depict the text.
Text	Poster includes a fact about taking care of library books.	Poster includes a fact about taking care of library books.	Poster includes a fact about taking care of library books.	Poster does not include a fact about taking care of library books.
Attractiveness	The poster is exceptionally attractive.	The poster is somewhat attractive.	The poster is a little messy.	The poster is very messy.

Extension Idea

When a class visits the library for checkout time, choose a few students to be the Library Patrol Deputies. Explain that they are responsible for straightening the library media center as their class looks for books and then exits. Chosen students wear Deputy badges (page 38).

WANTED

Scribbling Sam

$10,000 Reward

For rounding up this lowdown
library outlaw.

WANTED

Ripping Ryan

$10,000 Reward

For rounding up this lowdown
library outlaw.

WANTED

Bookworm Brittany

$10,000 Reward

For rounding up this lowdown
library outlaw.

WANTED

Overdue Olivia

$10,000 Reward

For rounding up this lowdown
library outlaw.

WANTED

Abandon Alex

$10,000 Reward

For rounding up this lowdown
library outlaw.

Library Patrol Stickers

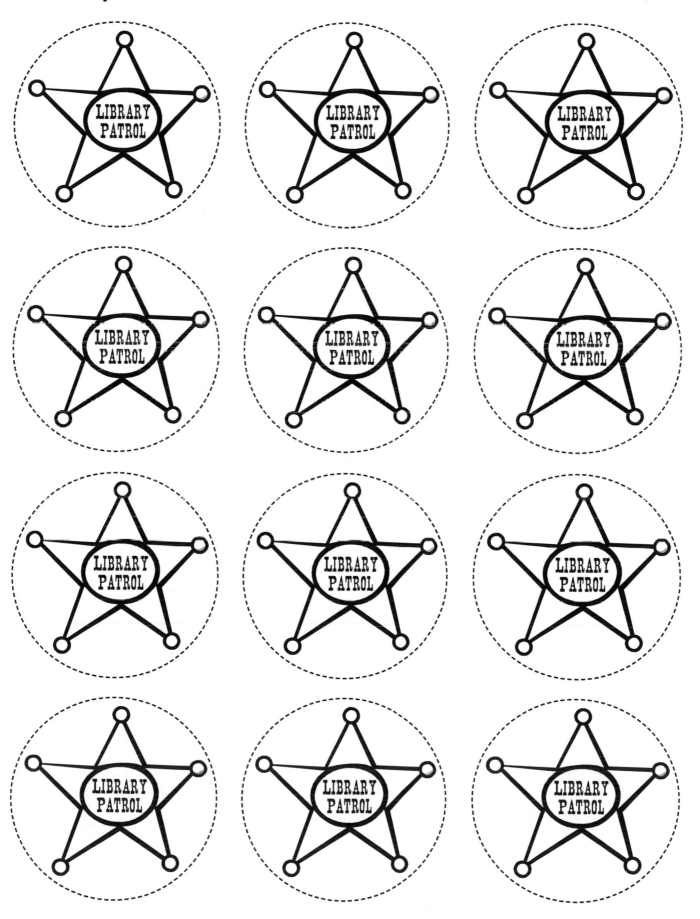

Library Patrol Bookmarks

Library Patrol Deputy Badges

Chapter 3

Chasing the Story
Teaching the Super3 and Big6

Lessons in this chapter incorporate use of the Super3 or the Big6, and can help your students learn the fundamentals of good research and reporting! Choose the research model appropriate for the age and experience of your students.

Grade Level: 3–5

Chapter Materials:

The following materials will be needed for each lesson in the chapter:

- Super3 or Big6 posters

Lesson 1: Hot off the Press

Time Required: 1 class period

Standards

1.1.1   Follow an inquiry-based process in seeking knowledge in curricular subjects, and make the real-world connection for using this process in own life.

1.1.3   Develop and refine a range of questions to frame the search for new understanding.

1.1.4   Find, evaluate, and select appropriate sources to answer questions.

1.1.9   Collaborate with others to broaden and deepen understanding.

Lesson Objectives

1.   Students will correctly identify steps of an information literacy model.

2.   Students will complete the first step of research through application of an information literacy model.

Additional Materials

- Top Reporter Story Ideas (page 44)

- Construction paper (one piece for every two students)

- White copy paper (two sheets per student, cut into quarters)

- Address labels

- Staplers

- Big6 posters

- Pencils

Preparation

1.   Purchase or borrow Big6 posters and display in library media center.

2.   Copy and distribute the Top Reporter Story Ideas sheet (one per small group).

3.   Cut the white copy paper into quarters. Cut the construction paper in half.

4.   Use the address labels to print a sticker for each student that says "Top Reporter Notebook."

Lesson Plan

1. Explain to students that they are going to become reporters. Reporters gather information on topics or events and share that information with the public. Every good reporter needs two things: their brains and a notebook for recording information.

2. Give each student the 8 quarters of copy paper and ½ a sheet of construction paper. Demonstrate for students how to stack the papers to form the inside of their notebooks. Then, show students how to fold their construction paper in half and place it around the copy paper to form a notebook. Help students staple their notebooks together. Give students a "Top Reporter" sticker to adhere to the front of their notebook.

3. Explain to students that every reporter follows steps for gathering information on a specific topic. As reporters, they are going to follow some very important directions, called research skills.

4. Utilize the posters to introduce the Big6 or Super3 to the students. As you summarize each step, have students record the steps on the first page of their notebooks.

5. Tell students that now that they have their brainpower, notebooks, and directions, they are ready to become top reporters!

6. Divide students into groups of 3–4 students. Hand out the Top Reporter Story Idea Sheet to each group. Have each group choose a topic to "report" on.

7. Have students complete the planning stages of the information literacy model they are following. (For the Super3, this step will be the Plan stage and for the Big6, this step will be Task Definition and Information Seeking Strategies.) Working together as a group, they should brainstorm resources available to help them gather information for their story. While brainstorming, students should record these ideas in their clue notebooks.

8. Collect clue notebooks for next lesson.

Lesson 2: Calling All Reporters

Time Required: 2 class periods

Standards

1.1.2 Follow an inquiry-based process in seeking knowledge in curricular subjects, and make the real-world connection for using this process in own life.

1.1.6 Read, view, and listen for information presented in any format (e.g., textual, visual, media, digital) in order to make inferences and gather meaning.

1.3.3 Follow ethical and legal guidelines in gathering and using information.

Lesson Objectives

1. Students will apply the steps of an information literacy model.

2. Students will utilize note-taking strategies to record information on a topic.

3. Students will follow legal guidelines by correctly citing resources.

Materials

- Pencils

- Top Reporter notebooks from previous lesson

- One Top Reporter tip sheet (page 45) per group

Lesson Plan

1. Utilize the posters to review the Big6 or Super3 with the students.

2. Pass the notebooks back to the students.

3. Explain to students that they are now ready to conduct the next steps of their Top Reporter directions. (For the Super3, this step will be the Do stage, and for the Big6, this will be the Location and Access stage.) They are going to hunt for information to help them present their story!

4. Give each group a Top Reporter Tip Sheet.

5. Have each group locate the resources they wrote down in the last class period.

6. Explain to students the importance of recording notes in one's own words to avoid plagiarism.

7. Teach students how to cite the resources that they utilize.

8. Begin researching information. Students will work together to locate information within the resources and record it in their reporter notebooks. Each group should also include the citation for their resource in their notebooks.

9. Collect notebooks for next lesson.

   (Note: This may require an additional class session.)

Lesson 3: Cracking the Case

Time Required: 1 class period

Standards

1.3.3 Follow ethical and legal guidelines in gathering and using information.

1.1.1 Continue an inquiry-based research process by applying critical- thinking skills (analysis, synthesis, evaluation, organization) to information and knowledge in order to construct new understandings, draw conclusions, and create new knowledge.

1.1.2 Organize knowledge so that it is useful.

2.1.5 Collaborate with others to exchange ideas, develop new understandings, make decisions, and solve problems.

Lesson Objectives

1. Students will apply the steps of an information literacy model.

2. Students will follow legal guidelines by correctly citing resources.

3. Students will select information to use in creating a poster.

4. Students will create a poster to share findings with the class.

Materials

- Top Reporter Tip Sheet (page 45)
- Pencils
- Top Reporter notebooks from previous lesson
- White construction paper or posterboard
- Crayons

Preparation

1. Copy Top Reporter Tip Sheet (one per group).

Lesson Plan

1. Utilize the posters to review the Big6 or Super3 with the students.

2. Pass the Top Reporter notebooks back to the students.

3. Explain to students that they are now ready to conduct the next steps of their Super Sleuth directions. (For the Super3, this step will be the Do stage, and for the Big6, this step will be the Use of Information and Synthesis stages.) They are ready to select the most important information to share!

4. Explain to students that reporters often follow tips to find information, and that not all information necessarily needs to be used in the final product. Good reporters will weed out information that is not helpful or relevant to their story, and use only what is needed to effectively present it. Today, like good reporters, students will go through the information that they recorded in their reporter notebooks and circle the best facts that they want to use in the final product that you are about to explain.

5. Explain to students that in the next lesson, they will be sharing their "news story" with the class. They will be creating a poster to use in their presentation, which will display a picture of the topic and the important facts that need to be shared. The poster should also cite the resource(s) that they used.

6. Give students time to create a poster of their conclusions from research.

   (Note: This may require an additional class session.)

Lesson 4: Press Conference

Time Required: 2 class periods

Standards

3.1.1 Conclude an inquiry-based research process by sharing new understandings and reflecting on the learning.

3.1.2 Participate and collaborate as members of a social and intellectual network of learners.

3.1.3 Use writing and speaking skills to communicate new understandings effectively.

3.4.1 Assess the processes by which learning was achieved in order to revise strategies and learn more effectively in the future.

3.4.2 Assess the quality and effectiveness of the learning product.

3.4.3 Assess own ability to work with others in a group setting by evaluating varied roles, leadership, and demonstrations of respect for other viewpoints.

Lesson Objectives

1. Students will apply the steps of an information literacy model.

2. Students will follow share findings with the class.

Materials

- One Top Reporter Evaluation Sheet (page 46) per student

- pencils

- Top Reporter notebooks from previous lesson

- white construction paper or posterboard

- crayons

Preparation

1. Copy the evaluation sheet (one copy per student).

Lesson Plan

1. Explain to students that they are now ready to conduct the final steps of their Top Reporter directions, in the Evaluation or Review stage. They are ready to share their news stories with the class!

2. Gather students in the reading area.

3. Review expected behaviors for being active, attentive listeners.

4. Have each group or student come to the front of the class. Students will share their poster and information with the class.

5. Hang posters for others to read.

6. Explain to students that part of being a reporter is reviewing your work and evaluating how you would complete it differently the next time. Give each student an evaluation sheet to complete.

7. Collect evaluation sheets for use in planning additional research units.

   (Note: This may require an additional class session.)

Poster Rubric

CATEGORY	4	3	2	1
Use of Class Time	Used time well during each class period. Focused on getting the project done. Never distracted others.	Used time well during each class period. Usually focused on getting the project done and never distracted others.	Used some of the time well during each class period. There was some focus on getting the project done but occasionally distracted others.	Did not use class time to focus on the project OR often distracted others.
Focus	The poster includes all required elements of a citation.	The poster includes some of the required elements of a citation.	The poster includes a few of the required elements of a citation.	No citation is included.
Call Number	All facts displayed on the poster are accurate and relevant to the topic.	Most of the facts displayed on the poster are accurate and relevant to the topic.	Some of the facts displayed on the poster are accurate and relevant to the topic.	None of the facts displayed on the poster are accurate and relevant to the topic.
Shelving	The poster is exceptionally attractive in terms of design, layout, and neatness.	The poster is attractive in terms of design, layout and neatness.	The poster is acceptably attractive though it may be a bit messy.	The poster is distractingly messy or very poorly designed. It is not attractive.

Extension Idea

Visit the Big6 website and download the materials for the Big 6 matching game (_www.big6. com/2002/12/11/new-game-match-the-big6%E2%84%A2-grades-3-6/_). A version for the Super3 is also available. Copy and laminate several sets. Allow students to play the game to review the steps in the information literacy models.

Top Reporter Story Ideas

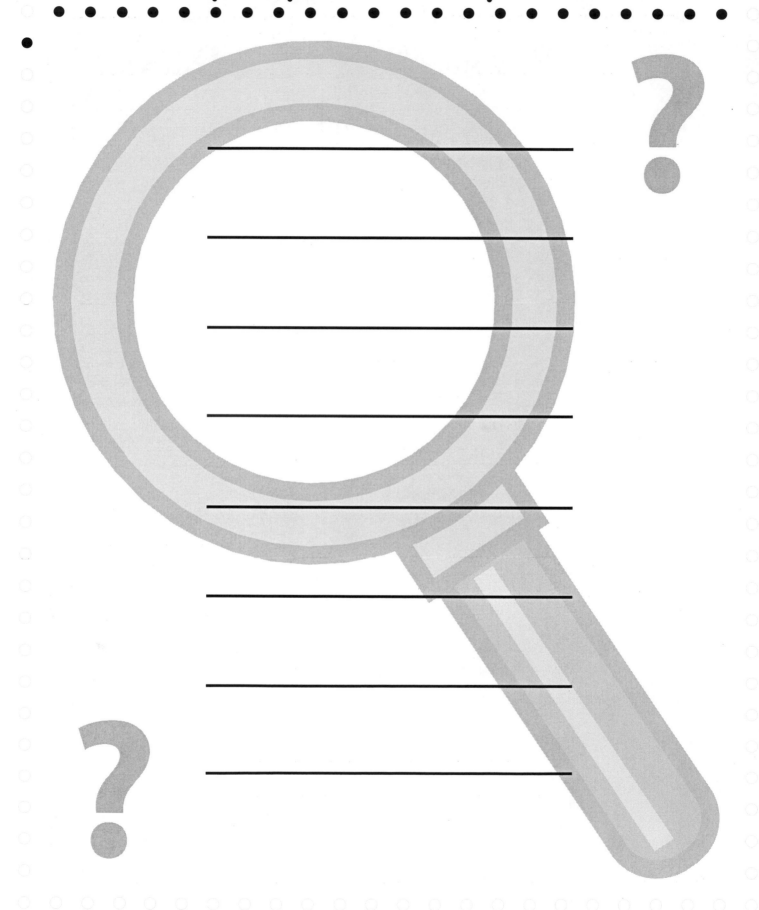

Top Reporter Tip Sheet

Top Reporter Evaluation

During this assignment,

- ☐ I worked to the best of my ability
- ☐ I felt comfortable looking up information
- ☐ I used my time wisely
- ☐ I did my best in creating the final product
- ☐ I felt comfortable presenting in front of my peers
- ☐ Other:

Top Reporter Evaluation

During this assignment,

- ☐ I worked to the best of my ability
- ☐ I felt comfortable looking up information
- ☐ I used my time wisely
- ☐ I did my best in creating the final product
- ☐ I felt comfortable presenting in front of my peers
- ☐ Other:

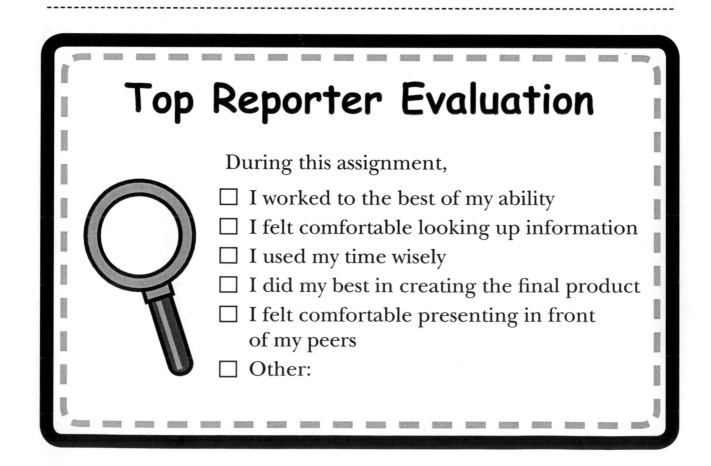

Chapter 4

The Secret Codes of Call Numbers

Make shelving easy and exciting for students by introducing them to the secret code of call numbers!

NOTE: In this chatper, I reference the "easy section" of the library. Other libraries may refer to this as the picture book section, or by another name entirely. This chapter can easily be tailored to your library by substituting my terminology with the language that best suits your instructional needs.

Grade Level: 2–3

Chapter Materials:

The following materials will be needed for each lesson in the chapter:

- Secret Code poster (page 51)
- laminating machine

Chapter Preparation:

- Copy the Secret Code posters and laminate.

Lesson 1: Writing Secret Codes

Time Required: 1 class period

Standards

1.1.3 Follow an inquiry-based process in seeking knowledge in curricular subjects, and make the real-world connection for using this process in own life.

1.1.3 Develop and refine a range of questions to frame the search for new understanding.

Lesson Objectives

1. Students will correctly identify how fiction and easy books are shelved in the library media center.

2. Students will demonstrate an understanding of how fiction and easy books are shelved in the library media center by accurately completing written activities.

Additional Materials

- Writing Secret Codes worksheet (page 52) and answer key (page 53)
- Writing Secret Codes poster (page 51)
- Sample fiction book
- Sample easy book
- Dry erase board
- Dry erase markers
- Laminating machine

Lesson Preparation

- Copy the Writing Secret Code worksheet (one per student).

Lesson Plan

1. Gather students in the fiction section.

2. Review with students the difference between fiction and nonfiction books.

3. Ask students to point out the easy section of the library media center. Explain that the easy section contains special fiction books. They are also make-believe but are mainly picture books. Books in the fiction section are typically chapter books.

4. Ask students if they know how fiction and easy books are shelved. Is it by size? By color? By favorite authors? Give students time to brainstorm ideas.

5. After students generate several ideas, tell them that fiction and easy books are shelved by a secret code. That secret code is called "call numbers." In fact, every book wears its secret code on its spine. If the students know how to read and write the secret codes, they will always be able to find books in the library media center.

6. Tell students that they are going to learn how to read and write in library secret code.

7. Hold up the poster that demonstrates a fiction call number. Explain to students that this is a secret code for a fiction book. The "F" tells us that the book belongs in the fiction section of the library media center. The letters beneath the "F" indicate where in that section the book is shelved. Those letters are the first letters in the author's last name. Once in the fiction section, the books are in alphabetical order, so someone shelving it can quickly locate similar secret codes and put the book away.

8. Hold up the Writing Secret Code poster. Explain to students that this is a secret code for an easy book. The "E" tells us that the book belongs in the easy section of the library media center. The letters beneath the "E" indicate where in that section the book is shelved. Those letters are the first letters in the author's last name. Once in the easy section, the books are in alphabetical order, so someone shelving it can quickly locate similar secret codes and put the book away.

9. Using the dry erase board, tell students that there is a pattern for writing the secret code. The first line is where the book belongs in the library. The second line is typically the first three letters of the author's last name.

10. Hold up the sample fiction book. Ask students to help you write the secret code for the book. Repeat with the easy book.

11. Tell students that they are going to practice writing in secret code.

12. Give students a worksheet and allow them the remaining class time to complete.

13. Collect worksheets for next lesson.

Lesson 2: Reading Secret Codes

Time Required: 1 class period

Standards

1.1.1 Follow an inquiry-based process in seeking knowledge in curricular subjects, and make the real-world connection for using this process in own life.

1.1.3 Develop and refine a range of questions to frame the search for new understanding.

Lesson Objectives

1. Students will correctly identify how fiction and easy books are shelved in the library media center.

2. Students will demonstrate an understanding of how fiction and easy books are shelved in the library media center by accurately completing written activities.

Additional Materials

- Reading Secret Codes worksheet (page 54) and answer key (page 55)

- Writing Secret Codes worksheet from previous lesson

Lesson Preparation

- Copy the reading secret codes worksheet (one per student).

Lesson Plan

1. Gather students in the fiction section of the library.

2. Using the posters from Lesson 1, review with students the secret code for shelving fiction and easy books. Review with students the pattern for writing secret codes.

3. Pass back Writing Secret Codes worksheet from previous lesson. Review answers with students.

4. Congratulate students on a job well done. Tell them that since they know how to write secret codes, you feel that they will now be able to read secret codes.

5. Review with students what each line of a call number represents. Show students where to find call numbers on a book by pointing out the spine label on several books. Explain to students that all books in the library media center have this secret code.

6. Give each student a reading secret codes worksheet.

7. Give students time to complete worksheet.

8. Review answers in class.

Lesson 3: Organizing Secret Codes

Time Required: 1 class period

Standards

1.1.2 Use prior and background knowledge as context for new learning.

3.1.2 Participate and collaborate as members of a social and intellectual network of learners.

3.2.3 Demonstrate teamwork by working productively with others.

Lesson Objectives

1. Students will correctly identify how fiction and easy books are shelved in alphabetical order in the library media center.

2. Students will demonstrate an understanding of how fiction and easy books are shelved in the library media center by participating in a team activity.

Additional Materials

• Secret Code Game Cards (page 56–59)

• cardstock

Lesson Preparation

• Copy the secret code game cards onto cardstock. Cut apart and laminate.

Lesson Plan

1. Gather students in the fiction section of the library.

2. Using the poster from Lesson 1, review the secret code for shelving fiction and easy books, and the pattern for writing secret codes.

3. Explain to students that once the secret code has been figured out, the person who shelves the book needs to place it in the right area. To do that, all secret codes are arranged in alphabetical order by the bottom line of the secret code. So, secret codes that start with an "A" on the bottom line will come near the beginning of that section, while letters that start with a "Z" on the bottom line will come near the end of that section. Arranging the secret codes in alphabetical order makes putting away books quick and easy.

4. Explain to students that today, they will work in teams to read and organize secret codes. In order for their team to win, they must be excellent at reading secret codes and paying attention to the bottom line of the secret code.

5. Explain to students that they will each be given a game card. On the card is a secret code. Some of the secret codes are for fiction books and some are for easy books. When play begins, they must first group with other students who have the same type of secret code. Then, they must all arrange themselves in correct alphabetical order according to their secret codes. The first group to do so is the winner.

6. Give each student a game card and begin play.

7. Once students are done arranging their teammates, call time and check their work.

8. Continue playing the game as time allows.

Lesson 4: Using Secret Codes in the Library Media Center

Time Required: 1 class period

Standards

1.1.2 Use prior and background knowledge as context for new learning.

1.4.3 Monitor gathered information, and assess for gaps or weaknesses.

1.4.4 Seek appropriate help when it is needed.

Lesson Objectives

1. Students will review how fiction and easy books are shelved in alphabetical order in the library media center.

2. Students will demonstrate an understanding of how fiction and easy books are shelved in the library media center by shelving books in the correct places.

Additional Materials

- Stack of fiction and easy books
- Shelf markers

Lesson Preparation

- Pull a stack of fiction and easy books to be shelved.

Lesson Plan

1. Gather students in the fiction section.

2. Using the poster from Lesson 1, review the secret code for shelving fiction and easy books. All secret codes are arranged in alphabetical order by the bottom line of the secret code. So, secret codes that start with an "A" on the bottom line will come near the beginning of that section while letters that start with a "Z" on the bottom line will come near the end of that section. Arranging the secret codes in alphabetical order makes putting away books quick and easy.

3. Tell students that you have a stack of fiction and easy books to be shelved. Since they have become proficient at reading secret codes, you wanted their assistance in shelving the books. Explain that you will give each student a shelf marker and a book. The students should read the secret code and then shelve the book. After they shelve the book, they should place their shelf marker next to it and raise their hand. You will come around and check their work on an individual basis.

4. Pass out shelf markers and books.

5. Supervise students as they work and check on them individually. For students who do not correctly shelve the book, review the secret code and assist them in finding the correct location for the book.

6. If time allows, play review game from previous lesson.

Shelving Books Rubric

CATEGORY	4	3	2	1
Call Numbers	Always identifies call number correctly.	Usually identifies call number correctly.	Rarely identifies call number correctly.	Never identifies call number correctly.
Shelving	Always shelves book correctly.	Usually shelves book correctly.	Rarely shelves book correctly.	Never shelves book correctly.
Time-management	Always uses time efficiently.	Usually uses time efficiently.	Rarely uses time efficiently.	Never uses time efficiently.

Extension Idea

Hook an LCD projector to a computer with access to the automated card catalog. Use a class session to teach students how to use the card catalog to search for available resources. Review with students how to identify the secret code, or call number, of those materials. Select books and have students work in teams to pull those books from the shelf.

Writing Secret Code

The top line tells where the book belongs.

This F means that this book would go in the FICTION section.

The bottom line tells what shelf the book belongs on within its section.

This RAN means that this book would go on the R shelf with other similar secret codes

The top line tells where the book belongs.

This E means that this book would go in the Easy section

The bottom line tells what shelf the book belongs on within its section.

This HAR means that this book would go on the H shelf with other similar secret codes.

Writing Secret Code Worksheet

Can you crack the secret code? Read the clues below. Then, write the secret code that would match the book described in the clue.

Clue #1   I am a fiction book written by Gary Paulsen.

_____

Clue #2   An author named Robert Munsch wrote this picture book.

_____

Clue #3   I am a chapter book whose author's name is Avi.

_____

Clue #4   I am an easy book by Arnold Lobel.

_____

Clue #5   An author named E. B. White wrote this chapter book.

_____

Clue #6   I am a book full of pictures who was written by Jan Brett.

_____

Clue #7   I am an easy book written by Eric Carle.

_____

Clue #8   Author Phyllis Reynolds Naylor wrote this chapter book.

_____

Clue #9   I am a fiction book written by J. K. Rowling.

_____

Clue #10 I am an easy book written by Dr. Seuss.

_____

Writing Secret Code Worksheet

Can you crack the secret code? Read the clues below. Then, write the secret code that would match the book described in the clue.

Clue #1   I am a fiction book written by Gary Paulsen.

   F Pau

Clue #2   An author named Robert Munsch wrote this picture book.

   E Mun

Clue #3   I am a chapter book whose author's name is Avi.

   F Avi

Clue #4   I am an easy book by Arnold Lobel.

   E Lob

Clue #5   An author named E. B. White wrote this chapter book.

   F Whi

Clue #6   I am a book full of pictures who was written by Jan Brett.

   E Bre

Clue #7   I am an easy book written by Eric Carle.

   E Car

Clue #8   Author Phyllis Reynolds Naylor wrote this chapter book.

   F Nay

Clue #9   I am a fiction book written by J. K. Rowling.

   F Row

Clue #10   I am an easy book written by Dr. Seuss.

   E Seu

Reading Secret Code Worksheet

Can you crack the secret code? Read the secret codes below. Write down the shelf and section of the library where the book belongs.

F Row	Section: Shelf:		**E Cro**	Section: Shelf:
E Ber	Section: Shelf:		**E Rit**	Section: Shelf:
E Num	Section: Shelf:		**F War**	Section: Shelf:
F Bro	Section: Shelf:		**F Nim**	Section: Shelf:
F Van	Section: Shelf:		**E Chi**	Section: Shelf:
E Zio	Section: Shelf:		**E Dar**	Section: Shelf:
F Hol	Section: Shelf:		**F Dit**	Section: Shelf:

Reading Secret Code Worksheet Answer Key

Reading Secret Code Worksheet

Can you crack the secret code? Read the secret codes below. Write down the shelf and section of the library where the book belongs.

F Row	Section:	**Fiction**
	Shelf:	**Rs**
E Ber	Section:	**Easy**
	Shelf:	**Bs**
E Num	Section:	**Easy**
	Shelf:	**Ns**
F Bro	Section:	**Fiction**
	Shelf:	**Bs**
F Van	Section:	**Fiction**
	Shelf:	**Vs**
E Zio	Section:	**Easy**
	Shelf:	**Zs**
F Hol	Section:	**Fiction**
	Shelf:	**Hs**

E Cro	Section:	**Easy**
	Shelf:	**Cs**
E Rit	Section:	**Easy**
	Shelf:	**Rs**
F War	Section:	**Fiction**
	Shelf:	**Ws**
F Nim	Section:	**Fiction**
	Shelf:	**Ns**
E Chi	Section:	**Easy**
	Shelf:	**Cs**
E Dar	Section:	**Easy**
	Shelf:	**Ds**
F Dit	Section:	**Fiction**
	Shelf:	**Ds**

Secret Code Game Cards

Secret Code	Secret Code	Secret Code
E Ran	E Hot	E Ber
Secret Code	**Secret Code**	**Secret Code**
E Zio	E Zie	E Bar
Secret Code	**Secret Code**	**Secret Code**
E Hof	E Hor	E Aar

Secret Code Game Cards

Secret Code E Oar	**Secret Code** E Num	**Secret Code** E Dit
Secret Code E Chi	**Secret Code** E Wet	**Secret Code** E Seu
Secret Code E All	**Secret Code** E Sar	**Secret Code** E Ide

Secret Code Game Cards

Secret Code	Secret Code	Secret Code
F Avi	F Dot	F Nay
Secret Code	Secret Code	Secret Code
F Whi	F War	F App
Secret Code	Secret Code	Secret Code
F Row	F Col	F Con

Secret Code Game Cards

Secret Code	Secret Code	Secret Code
F McC	F Tri	F Ter
Secret Code F Opp	**Secret Code** F Min	**Secret Code** F Eri
Secret Code F Fim	**Secret Code** F Lin	**Secret Code** F Lon

Chapter 5

Superheroes

Rescuing Nonfiction Books

Lessons in this chapter familiarize students with Dewey, and transform them into writers, storytellers, and nonfiction-shelving superheroes, too!

Grade Level: 3–4

Chapter Materials:

The following materials will be needed for each lesson in the chapter:

- Dewey Decimal Posters
- Laminating machine

Chapter Preparation:

- Laminate posters and hang in library media center.

Lesson 1: We Need a Hero

Time Required: 2 class periods

Standards

1.1.1 Follow an inquiry-based process in seeking knowledge in curricular subjects, and make the real-world connection for using this process in own life.

1.1.9 Collaborate with others to broaden and deepen understanding.

1.1.2 Organize knowledge so that it is useful.

2.1.5 Collaborate with others to exchange ideas, develop new understandings, make decisions, and solve problems.

Lesson Objectives

1. Students will correctly identify classifications of the Dewey Decimal system.

2. Students will create a fictitious character for a short story that depicts a classification of the Dewey Decimal system.

3. Students will work cooperatively with group members.

Lesson Materials

- Dewey Decimal Letter (page 65)
- Brainstorming Worksheet (page 66)

Lesson Preparation

1. Copy the Dewey Decimal Letter and practice reading aloud.

2. Copy brainstorming worksheet (one copy per group).

Lesson Plan

1. Gather students in the nonfiction section of the library media center.

2. Explain to them that in previous units, they have learned how fiction and easy books are shelved. Ask students to recall that information.

3. Announce to students that they are now ready to learn about shelving books in the nonfiction section. Tell them that just this

very day, you were putting books away in the nonfiction section, and you found a letter lying on the shelves. Hold up the story for students to see.

4. Read story aloud to students.

5. Challenge students to protect the nonfiction section from Mr. Chaos by becoming superheroes. Explain that they can be superheroes by using correct library behaviors, such as using shelf markers, putting books on the cart when they are ready to be shelved, and taking care of their books.

6. Tell students that in addition to their own heroic deeds, you want to create a superhero to protect each section of the nonfiction books. Tell them that they will be divided into small groups. Each group will be assigned a number in the Dewey Decimal system. Students must think of a superhero that could protect that particular section of books.

7. Explain to students that the nonfiction books are divided into 10 groups. Each group begins with a different number and contains a different type of book. Utilize the Dewey Decimal system posters to explain the 10 Dewey groups and what types of books are found in each category.

8. Divide students into 10 small groups and assign each group to a different section of the Dewey Decimal system.

9. Explain to students that their superhero must have a name, a special power, and a love for books in his or her specific section. Give students an example by brainstorming a superhero as a class. For instance, if a group is assigned the 500s, which includes science, they might develop a superhero named "The Professor" who can summon a team of dinosaurs and animals to protect the books. Or, he might be able to shoot lightening, sparks, and different types of precipitation from his fingertips to confuse his enemies. He would wear a cape with the number 5 since he protects the 500s and might also wear a lab coat and safety goggles as part of his costume. His favorite books might be *The Magic School Bus* series by Joanna Cole.

10. Give each group a brainstorming worksheet to develop their superheroes.

11. Give students remaining time to develop their superhero while assisting them with the task.

(Note: This may require an additional class session.)

Lesson 2: Superheroes to the Rescue

Time Required: 2 class periods

Standards

1.1.2 Organize knowledge so that it is useful.

2.1.5 Collaborate with others to exchange ideas, develop new understandings, make decisions, and solve problems.

3.1.3 Use writing and speaking skills to communicate new understandings effectively.

Lesson Objectives

1. Students will create a storyboard for a short story that depicts a classification of the Dewey Decimal system.

2. Students will utilize their storyboard to write a short story about a superhero saving the Dewey Decimal system.

3. Students will work cooperatively with group members.

Additional Materials

• Superhero Storyboard (page 67)

• Superhero Template (page 68)

Lesson Preparation

1. Copy Superhero Storyboard for students (one copy per group).

2. Copy superhero template for students (one copy per group).

Lesson Plan

1. Gather students in the nonfiction section of the library media center.

2. Review assignment of creating a superhero to protect the nonfiction books and Dewey Decimal system with the students. Explain that they will brainstorm a story that tells

everyone about how their superhero saves their section of books.

3. Explain to students how to utilize the storyboard to outline the beginning, middle, and end of their story. Remind them that their story must have a conflict that is resolved by the end of the story.

4. Give each group a storyboard.

5. Give students time to develop their storyboard and assist as necessary.

6. As students complete their storyboards, review them. Then, give each group the superhero template to begin writing their story.

(Note: This may require an additional class session.)

Lesson 3: Dewey by Day, Superheroes by Night

Time Required: 1 class period

Standards

1.1.2 Organize knowledge so that it is useful.

2.1.6 Collaborate with others to exchange ideas, develop new understandings, make decisions, and solve problems.

3.1.3 Use writing and speaking skills to communicate new understandings effectively.

Lesson Objectives

1. Students will practice reading aloud a short story with effective diction, voice projection, and sound effects.

2. Students will work cooperatively with group members.

Additional Materials

- Dewey Decimal short story from Lesson 1
- posterboard (one per group)
- markers or crayons

Lesson Plan

1. Gather students in the nonfiction section of the library media center.

2. Review their assignment to create a superhero to protect the nonfiction books and Dewey Decimal system with the students. Explain that they will begin practicing reading their story aloud.

3. Using the Dewey Decimal short story as an example, read aloud in a variety of tones, including a soft whisper, a bored tone, rapid speech, and other common presentation styles completed by students. Ask students to evaluate each of these storytelling styles. Which of them, if any, are effective and interesting? Which are easy to understand?

4. Reread the tale using a style that requires vocal projection and adds excitement to the story. Ask students to evaluate that style. Explain that this is how you would like each of their stories read aloud to classmates. It should include clear diction, strong projection, and varied inflections to make the story interesting to the audience. One or more group members can read the story. Or, one group member may read the story while others make sound effects.

5. Have students divide into groups.

6. Give students remaining time to practice presenting their stories orally.

7. Give each group a piece of posterboard and either markers or crayons. Have students create a poster that depicts their superhero and the Dewey Decimal classification that he or she represents.

Lesson 4: Starring ... Superheroes !

Time Required: 1 class period

Standards

3.1.3 Use writing and speaking skills to communicate new understandings effectively.

3.2.1 Demonstrate leadership and confidence by presenting ideas to others in both formal and informal situations.

3.2.2 Show social responsibility by participating actively with others in learning situations and by contributing questions and ideas during group discussions.

Lesson Objectives

1. Students will share superhero short stories by reading them to the class.

2. Students will demonstrate respect for classmates by being active, attentive listeners during sharing of folktales.

Materials

- superhero short stories from previous lesson
- fabric in two colors (one dark and one light)
- stools

Preparation

1. Set stool or chair at the head of the reading area.

2. Cut the dark fabric to look like a cape.

3. Use the light fabric to cut a large "S". Glue the large S to the dark fabric to create a superhero cape.

Lesson Plan

1. Explain to students that this is the day they will get to share their short stories with their classmates!

2. Have each group take out their short stories for presentation.

3. Gather students in the reading area.

4. Review expected behaviors for being active, attentive listeners.

5. Have each group come to the front of the class. As students take turns presenting their stories, have the lead reader wear the superhero cape. Ask the other students to first hold up the poster and explain who their superhero is and what section of the Dewey Decimal system is represented. Then, have the group present their story to the class.

6. Hang poster and stories in the nonfiction shelves for others to read.

Short Story Rubric

CATEGORY	4	3	2	1
Classification	The Dewey Decimal system classification is integrated fully in the story.	The Dewey Decimal system classification is mostly integrated in the story.	The Dewey Decimal system classification is somewhat integrated in the story.	The Dewey Decimal system classification is not integrated at all in the story.
Organization	The story is very well organized.	The story is pretty well organized.	The story is a little hard to follow.	Ideas seem to be randomly arranged.
Solution/Resolution	The solution is easy to understand.	The solution is easy to understand, and is somewhat logical.	The solution is a little hard to understand.	No solution is attempted or it is impossible to understand.
Superhero	The superhero is creative and accurately represents the Dewey Decimal classification.	The superhero is creative and somewhat represents the Dewey Decimal classification.	The superhero is somewhat creative and somewhat represents the Dewey Decimal classification.	The superhero is not creative and does not represent the Dewey Decimal classification.

Extension Idea

Provide students with craft materials and fabric to make capes and other costumes to represent their superheroes. Have students practice acting out the story using facial expression, gestures, and blocking. Then, have students act out the story for younger classes to introduce them to the nonfiction section of the library and the location of various topics of books.

Help! My name is Dashing Dewey. Haven't heard of me? Well, I'm the superhero who shelves nonfiction books with lightning fast speed! I'm the one who organizes all of the true books in your library! I dash around so quickly that I appear invisible! That's probably why you don't realize that I exist!

I need your help. A very bad man, Mr. Chaos, wants to destroy your library—specifically, the nonfiction books! He wants to throw them all on the floor, rip pages out, and mix them up so that no one will ever be able to find their favorite topics again! His goal is create so much chaos and disorganization that students will stop using the library.

You're probably asking, how can we help? Why, by assisting me in the creation of a team of superheroes that will defend the nonfiction section! With a whole team of superheroes ready to shelve books, Mr. Chaos won't stand a chance! Will you be superheroes too? Can you learn how to shelve nonfiction books so that you can help the superheroes? I hope so. I'm counting on you!

—*Dashing Dewey*

Superhero

Name: _____

Dewey Decimal Number _____

Superpowers: _____

_____

_____

Description: _____

_____

_____

_____

_____

_____

_____

_____

Favorite Books: _____

_____

_____

_____

Superhero Storyboard

Beginning	Main Event #1	Problem/Conflict

Main Event #2	Main Event #3	Solution

Starring... Superheroes !

Chapter 6
All-Star Biographies

Students will learn the elements of biographies and test their wits and athletic skills in these all-star library lessons.

Grade Level: 2–3

Chapter Materials:

The following materials will be needed for each lesson in the chapter:

- Biography jersey posters (page 74–78)
- Laminating machine
- Copy paper in school colors
- Fishing line
- Tag board
- Markers

Chapter Preparation:

1. Copy the biography jersey posters on copy paper in school colors. Make two sets.
2. Laminate and cut out the posters.
3. Use the fishing line to hang one set of the posters from the ceiling so that they dangle above the biography section of your library media center. The second set will be used during the lesson.
4. Make a banner that says "All-Star Team" and post on the biography section shelving.
5. In the biography section, create a display of biographies about sports stars for students to check out.

Lesson 1: Get Your Head in the Game

Time Required: 1 class period

Standards

1.1.5 Evaluate information found in selected sources on the basis of accuracy, validity, appropriateness for needs, importance, and social and cultural context.

1.1.6 Read, view, and listen for information presented in any format (e.g., textual, visual, media, digital) in order to make inferences and gather meaning.

1.4.3 Monitor gathered information, and assess for gaps or weaknesses.

Lesson Objectives

1. Students will correctly identify elements of the biography genre.

2. Students will listen to a reading of an age-appropriate biography and correctly recall elements of a biography included in the book.

Additional Materials

- Age-appropriate sports biography
- Biographies of movie stars, singers, athletes, and other pop culture icons
- Foam basketball and hoop

Lesson Preparation

- Hang the basketball hoop in the biography section at a height that students can easily reach.

Lesson Plan

1. Gather students in the biography section of the library media center.

2. Explain to them that they are going to study the biography genre. Ask if they know what biographies are and give them time to recall prior knowledge.

3. Explain that a biography is an account of a person's life, usually a famous person, written by another person. Sometimes, famous people decide to write a biography about themselves. When they do that, the books are called autobiographies. Biographies are books that are true, so they are non-fiction.

4. Show students the sports biographies on display in the biography section. Booktalk the materials to pique students' interest and remind them that they can check out these materials to read more about their favorite sports stars.

5. Explain that biographies are like all-stars on a sports team. To become an all-star, the athlete has to work hard, practice, and always put their best effort into a game. Once they excel at their sport, they might be called an "all-star" to indicate just how good they are. Biographies tell us about all-stars, but not just sports all-stars. Explain to students that biographies tell us about all-stars in music, movies, history, and more!

6. Introduce the elements of a biography. Hold up each jersey template and discuss why it is important to know this information about a person.

7. Read and discuss an age-appropriate sports biography. Tell students to pay close attention because after reading, they are going to play Biography Basketball and to win, they will need the information from the book.

8. Review book with students.

9. Explain how to play Biography Basketball. It is played teacher against students. To play, you will ask a question about the book or about the elements of a biography. Then, you will toss the basketball to a student, who must answer the question correctly without help from his/her teammates. If the students answer correctly, they get to shoot a basket and try to earn a point for their class. Each basket is worth 2 points. If the student answers incorrectly, the teacher gets to answer the question and try to shoot a basket to earn the points. Hard questions will be called "three-pointers." Teammates can be "fouled out" for blurting out answers and not raising their hand to answer the question.

10. Play game. Questions include:

    a. Are biographies fiction or nonfiction?

    b. What does the word nonfiction mean?

    c. Does the person who the biography is about write this book?

    d. What is a biography called when someone writes it about himself or herself?

    e. Can biographies be written about people other than sports stars?

    f. Biographies include five things about a person. Name one of them.

    g. Who was this book written about?

    h. When was he/she born?

    i. When did he/she die?

    j. What did he/she do that is significant?

Lesson 2: Score with Teamwork

Time Required: 2 class periods

Standards

1.1.5 Evaluate information found in selected sources on the basis of accuracy, validity, appropriateness for needs, importance, and social and cultural context.

1.1.6 Read, view, and listen for information presented in any format (e.g., textual, visual, media, digital) in order to make inferences and gather meaning.

3.1.2 Participate and collaborate as members of a social and intellectual network of learners.

3.2.2 Show social responsibility by participating actively with others in learning situations and by contributing questions and ideas during group discussions.

3.2.3 Demonstrate teamwork by working productively with others.

Lesson Objectives

1. Students will correctly identify elements of the biography genre.

2. Students will read and evaluate an age-appropriate biography.

3. Students will work collaboratively with classmates to present their findings to the class.

Additional Materials

- 5-6 age-appropriate biographies about athletes

- One Most Valuable Player worksheet (page 79) per group

- pencils

Lesson Preparation

1. Divide class roster in groups of 3-4.

2. Copy the Most Valuable Player worksheet. (one per group)

Lesson Plan

1. Gather students in the biography section next to the "All-Star Team" banner you created.

2. Ask students to recall what they remember about biographies from the previous lesson. Give students time to answer.

3. Review elements of a biography by holding up the jersey templates from the previous lesson. Ask students to recount what information is included in each element and why it is important to know that information in a biography.

4. Tell students that you are assembling an "All-Star Team" of biographies. These biographies will be placed in a special display for other students to see. Then, everyone will be able to learn more about biographies just as they are doing. Tell students that you need help assembling the "All-Star Team."

5. Explain that you will divide the students into groups of 3-4. Each group will be given one biography to read. They will read the book together. Then, they will fill out a scorecard on that biography. At the end of class, each group will discuss their biography and share whether or not they think it belongs on the "All-Star Team."

6. Divide students into groups. Give each group a pencil, a Most Valuable Player worksheet, an age-appropriate biography about an athlete.

7. Give groups time to read and fill out their worksheet while you monitor their behavior and provide assistance. Save worksheets for use in next lesson.

   (Note: This may require an additional class session.)

Lesson 3: Game Day

Time Required: 1 class period

Standards

3.1.2 Participate and collaborate as members of a social and intellectual network of learners.

3.2.2 Show social responsibility by participating actively with others in learning situations and by contributing questions and ideas during group discussions.

3.2.3 Demonstrate teamwork by working productively with others.

Lesson Objectives

1. Students will correctly identify elements of the biography genre.

2. Students will work collaboratively with classmates to present their findings to the class.

Materials

- Most Valuable Player worksheets from previous lesson

- Voting Cards (page 80)

- pencils

Lesson Preparation

- Copy the Voting Cards (one per student).

Lesson Plan

1. Gather students in the biography section next to the "All-Star Team" poster.

2. Ask students to recall what they remember about biographies from the previous lesson. Give students time to answer.

3. Review elements of a biography by holding up the jersey templates from the previous lesson. Ask students to recount what information is included in that element and why it is important to know that information in a biography.

4. Tell students that it is time to assemble our "All-Star Team."

5. Each group will present the biography it read and whether or not they feel it should be on the "All-Star Team" in the biography section. At the end of class, everyone will vote and select the members of the "All-Star Team." The books that earn the highest amount of votes will be placed in a special display.

6. Give each student a voting card and pencil. As each group introduces their biography, the students should record it on their voting card.

7. Have each group come to the front of the room and present their biography and evaluation.

8. Give students time to vote.

9. Calculate results and announce winners.

10. Pull those biographies and create a display in the biography section.

Most Valuable Player Rubric

CATEGORY	4	3	2	1
Voting	Students accurately and completely fill out the voting ballot to evaluate their classmates' presentations.	Students fill out the voting ballot with little omissions to evaluate their classmates' presentations.	Students fill out the voting ballot with many omissions to evaluate their classmates' presentations.	Students do not fill out the voting ballot with little omissions to evaluate their classmates' presentations.
Listening Skills	Students listen quietly without any interruptions.	Students listen quietly with one or two interruptions.	Students listen quietly with many interruptions.	Students do not listen quietly and frequently interrupt.
Teamwork	All students listen to teammates and participate in their group.	Most students listen to teammates and participate in their group.	Few students listen to teammates and participate in their group.	No students listen to teammates and participate in their group.
Worksheet	All sections of the worksheet are completed.	Most sections of the worksheet are completed.	Few sections of the worksheet are completed.	No sections of the worksheet are completed.

Extension Idea

Create a bulletin board with the heading "All-Star Biographies." Assign students to read a biography that is of interest to them. After reading the biography, students will complete a "stats sheet" (page 81) about the book. The "stats sheet" will be hung on the bulletin board to advertise available books in the biography section.

Biographies are Nonfiction (true) books

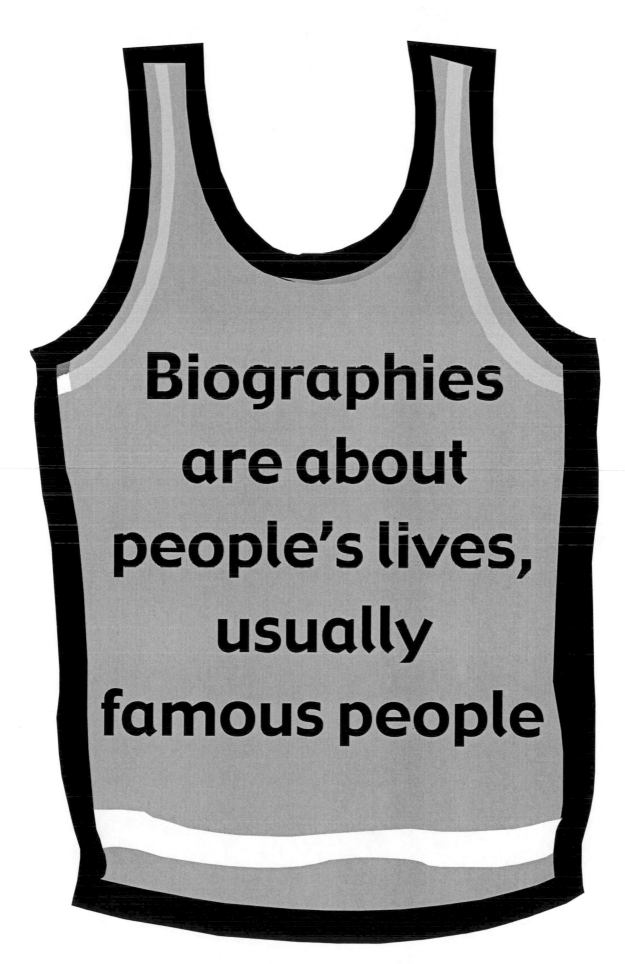

Biographies are about people's lives, usually famous people

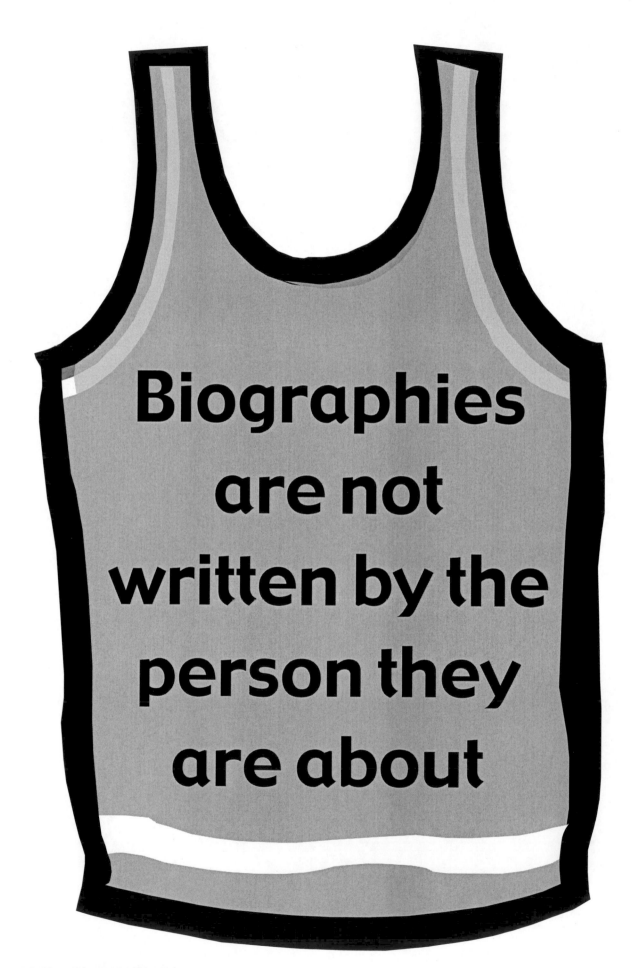

Biographies are not written by the person they are about

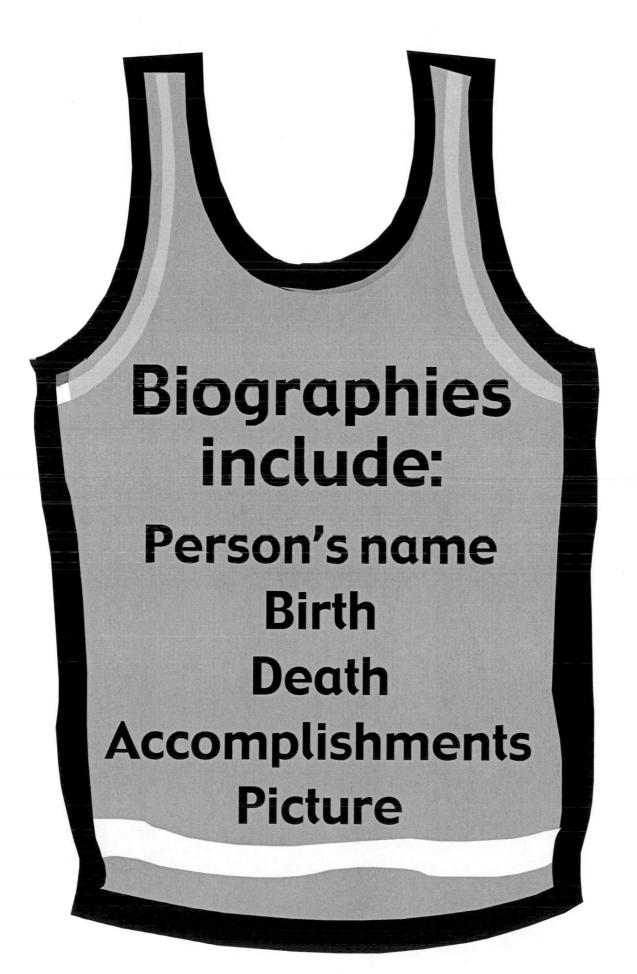

Biographies include:
Person's name
Birth
Death
Accomplishments
Picture

All-Star Biographies

MOST VALUABLE PLAYER

Title of Book

_____

Author's Name

_____

Did this biography...	Yes	No
Include the person's name?		
Include the person's birth?		
Include the person's death?		
Include why the person was famous?		
Include a picture or photo of the person?		
Was it interesting to read?		
Was it true and full of facts?		
SCORE		

I would / would not choose this book as a member of the All-Star team.

ALL-STAR TEAM VOTING SHEET

Title of Book	Yes	No

ALL-STAR TEAM VOTING SHEET

Title of Book	Yes	No

STATS SHEET

Book Title

_____

Author

_____

Name of famous person

_____

Birth   Death

_____   _____

Why this person is famous

_____

_____

_____

This book is

_____

_____ !

Chapter 7
Walk of Fame
Biographies

Roll out the red carpet, because the stars are out in your library! Through these lessons, students will review the elements of biographical writing and try it out, themselves. Even Hollywood has never seen anything quite like this!

Grade Level: 4–5

Chapter Materials:

- Elements of biographies star posters (pages 88–96)
- Yellow paper
- Laminating machine
- Fishing line

Chapter Preparation:

1. Copy the biography elements star templates on yellow paper. Make two sets.
2. Laminate and cut out the posters.
3. Use the fishing line to hang one set of the stars from the ceiling so that they dangle above the biography section of your library media center. The second set will be used during the lesson.
4. Make a banner that says "Walk of Fame" and post on the biography section shelving.
5. In the biography section, create a display of biographies about movie stars, singers, athletes and other pop culture icons for students to view and check out.

Lesson 1: Seeing Stars

Time Required: One 30-minute class period

Standards

1.1.5 Evaluate information found in selected sources on the basis of accuracy, validity, appropriateness for needs, importance, and social and cultural context.

1.1.6 Read, view, and listen for information presented in any format (e.g., textual, visual, media, digital) in order to make inferences and gather meaning.

1.4.3 Monitor gathered information, and assess for gaps or weaknesses.

Lesson Objectives

1. Students will correctly identify elements of the biography genre.
2. Students will listen to a reading of an age-appropriate biography and correctly recall elements of a biography included in the book.

Additional Materials

- Age-appropriate biography, such as *Wilma Unlimited* by Kathleen Krull

- Biographies of movie stars, singers, athletes, and other pop culture icons

- Biography review worksheet (page 97)

Preparation

1. Copy the biography review worksheet. (one per student)

Lesson Plan

1. Gather students in the biography section of the library media center.

2. Explain that they are going to study the biography genre. Ask them if they know what biographies are and give them time to recall prior knowledge.

3. Explain that a biography is an account about a person's life written by another person. Usually, biographies are about famous people, though there are times when "regular" people have biographies written about them. Sometimes, people decide to write a biography about themselves. When someone does that, it is called an autobiography.

4. Show students several popular biographies from the display in the biography section. Booktalk the materials to pique their interest.

5. Explain that these people are recognized in a place called the Hollywood Walk of Fame. On the Walk of Fame a star lists their name and a picture of the category that they contributed to, such as singing, movies, etc. It is a method of recognizing their fame and hard work in their occupation.

6. Explain that a biography section in a library is similar to the Hollywood Walk of Fame. Since not everyone can be in the Hollywood Walk of Fame, biographies teach others about the lives and and work of even more people who have contributed to society in some way. Biographies are just like the stars on that famous Hollywood sidewalk. That's why the biography section

is decorated with stars and a banner that says "Walk of Fame."

7. Tell students that outstanding biographies, such as the ones on display, have common elements. Introduce the each elements of a biography. Hold up each star shape and discuss why it is important to know this information about a person. Explain that most books in the biography genre include these elements and these elements separate them from other genres.

8. Read and discuss an age-appropriate biography about a pop culture icon, such as *Wilma Unlimited* by Kathleen Krull.

9. Pass out the biography review worksheet and have students complete it.

10. Review answers as a class.

11. Review with students what a biography is, common elements of a biography, and how the book read in class included those elements.

Lesson 2: Star Search

Standards

1.1.1 Follow an inquiry-based process in seeking knowledge in curricular subjects, and make the real-world connection for using this process in own life.

2.1.2 Organize knowledge so that it is useful.

3.1.2 Participate and collaborate as members of a social and intellectual network of learners.

3.2.2 Show social responsibility by participating actively with others in learning situations and by contributing questions and ideas during group discussions.

3.2.3 Demonstrate teamwork by working productively with others.

Lesson Objectives

1. Students will correctly identify elements of the biography genre.

2. Students will utilize the elements of the biography genre to interview a classmate.

3. Students will complete all interview questions by accurately recording classmate's thoughts, experiences, and opinions.

Materials

- Biography element posters (page 88–96)
- Yellow paper
- Laminator
- Blank lined paper OR Start Search Interview worksheet (page 98)
- Photograph of the Hollywood Walk of Fame

Preparation

1. Copy the interview worksheet (one per student).

2. Locate a photograph of the Hollywood Walk of Fame online and print for use in the lesson.

Lesson Plan

1. Gather students in the biography section next to the "Walk of Fame" poster.

2. Ask students to recall what they remember about biographies from the previous lesson. Give them time to answer.

3. Review the elements of a biography by holding up the star shapes from the previous lesson. Ask students to recount what information is included in that element and why it is important to know that information in a biography.

4. Show students the picture of the Hollywood Walk of Fame and explain that it is the way that movie stars, singers, and others are honored. Remind them that it was discussed in the last class session.

5. Explain to students that you think they all belong in the library's "Walk of Fame." Though biographies are typically about famous people, sometimes biographies are written about "regular" people. So, each student is going to write a biography to be included in the library's "Walk of Fame."

6. Explain to students that they are going to create a class "Walk of Fame" that will run from the library media center door to the biography section. The "Walk of Fame" will show the entire school what great students they are and encourage other people to learn about biographies.

7. Explain that each student will be assigned a partner to interview. As they interview, they will record answers for each element of a biography, such as job, life experiences, family, etc. In future lessons, they will write a biography about that person and be graded on their inclusion of all elements of a biography. Therefore, conducting a good interview is crucial to writing a quality biography.

8. Have students brainstorm questions that they might ask someone in an interview. As students list questions, write them on the board.

9. With students' help, determine which of the brainstormed questions address the elements of a biography. Have students write these questions on lined paper to use while interviewing their partner.

   (Note: If time does not allow for steps 7-8, use the Start Search Interview worksheet)

10. Assign partners.

11. Provide students with time to interview one another.

    (Note: This may require an additional class session.)

12. Collect interview sheets for use in the next lesson.

Lesson 3: Shining Stars

Standards

2.1.2 Organize knowledge so that it is useful.

2.2.4 Demonstrate personal productivity by completing products to express learning.

3.1.2 Participate and collaborate as members of a social and intellectual network of learners.

3.1.3 Use writing and speaking skills to communicate new understandings effectively.

3.3.4 Create products that apply to authentic, real-world contexts.

Lesson Objectives

1. Students will utilize elements of a biography to write a biography about a classmate.

2. Students will organize information in a logical manner.

3. Students will write to create a finished biography to share with classmates.

Materials

- Interviews from previous lesson

- Biography worksheet (page 99)

- 12" x 18" black construction paper

- Glue

Preparation

1. Copy the biography worksheet (one per student).

Lesson Plan

1. Gather students in the biography section next to the "Walk of Fame" poster.

2. Ask students to recall what they remember about biographies from the previous lesson. Give them time to answer.

3. Review the elements of a biography by holding up the star shapes from the previous lesson. Ask students to recount what information is included in that element and why it is important to know that information in a biography.

4. Remind students that you are going to create a class Walk of Fame that will run from the door to the biography section. That way, the entire school can see what great students they are and learn more about the biography genre.

5. Explain that they will utilize the information from their interviews to write a biography about their classmates.

6. Review writing ideas with students.

   a. They do not have to include every piece of information they found. Instead, they should select the most important or interesting information for their biographies.

   b. They should utilize each element of a biography while writing.

   c. The information should be arranged in logical format, such as chronological order.

7. Give each student a biography worksheet.

8. Give students class time to write their biographies. As they do, confer with them on their writing.

   (Note: This may require an additional class session.)

9. Give each student a piece of 12" x 18" black construction paper. Have students turn the paper vertically and paste their biography to the top half of the construction paper. The bottom half should remain blank for the next lesson.

10. Collect biographies for use in next lesson.

Lesson 4: Walk of Fame

Standards

3.1.4 Use writing and speaking skills to communicate new understandings effectively.

3.2.2 Demonstrate leadership and confidence by presenting ideas to others in both formal and informal situations.

3.2.2 Show social responsibility by participating actively with others in learning situations and by contributing questions and ideas during group discussions.

Lesson Objectives

1. Students will share written products by reading them to the class.

2. Students will demonstrate respect for classmates by being active, attentive listeners during sharing of biographies.

Materials

- Biographies from previous lesson
- Red bulletin board paper
- White tempera paint
- Paper plates
- Paper towels
- Digital camera
- "Walk of Fame" poster (page 101)

Preparation

1. Roll red bulletin board paper in front of the reading area and down the middle to look like a red carpet.

2. Place a paper plate on each table and pour a small amount of white tempera paint onto each paper plate.

3. Place a paper towel at each student's seat.

Lesson Plan

1. Explain to students that this is the day they get to hang their stars in the class "Walk of Fame"! Tell them that celebrities celebrate when their stars are placed in the Hollywood Walk of Fame. They walk down a red carpet, get their picture taken, and enjoy compliments. Today, we are going to celebrate just like the celebrities with our Biography Party!

2. Pass back biographies from previous lesson to the authors.

3. Gather students in the reading area.

4. Introduce a student and have them walk down the red carpet to stand in front of the class. Take their picture.

5. Have that student's partner read the biography they wrote to explain to the class why this person belongs in the Walk of Fame.

6. After reading the biographies, have students return to their seats.

7. Have each partner give the biography to the person about whom it is written.

8. Have students lightly place hands in the tempera paint and make handprints on the bottom half of their posters.

9. Allow posters to dry.

10. Print a picture of each student and adhere to poster.

11. After the handprints are dry, students may hang their biographies from the library media center door to the biography section to create their "Walk of Fame". At the beginning of the "Walk of Fame", hang the "Walk of Fame" poster to explain it to library media center visitors.

Biography Rubric

CATEGORY	4	3	2	1
Organization	Information is organized in a chronological manner.	Information is mainly organized in a chronological manner.	Information is somewhat organized in a chronological manner.	The information appears to be disorganized.
Interview	All questions are answered with supporting details.	Most questions are answered with supporting details.	Few questions are answered with supporting details.	No questions are answered with supporting details.
Reporting of Information	Information clearly relates to interview and assignment. It contains several supporting details.	Information mostly relates to interview and assignment. It contains some supporting details.	Information relates to interview and assignment. It contains no supporting details.	Information does not relate to interview and assignment. It contains no supporting details.
Mechanics	No spelling or punctuation errors.	Almost no spelling or punctuation errors.	A few spelling or punctuation errors.	Many spelling or punctuation errors.

Extension Idea

Create a bulletin board with the heading "Star Search: Check Out the Stars in Our Biography Section." Assign students to read a biography that is of interest to them. After reading the biography, students will complete a book review (page 100). The book review will be hung on the bulletin board to advertise available books in the biography section.

Name
of
Person

Birth

(where & when)

Life
Experiences

Death
(where & when)

Why Famous

Job

Family

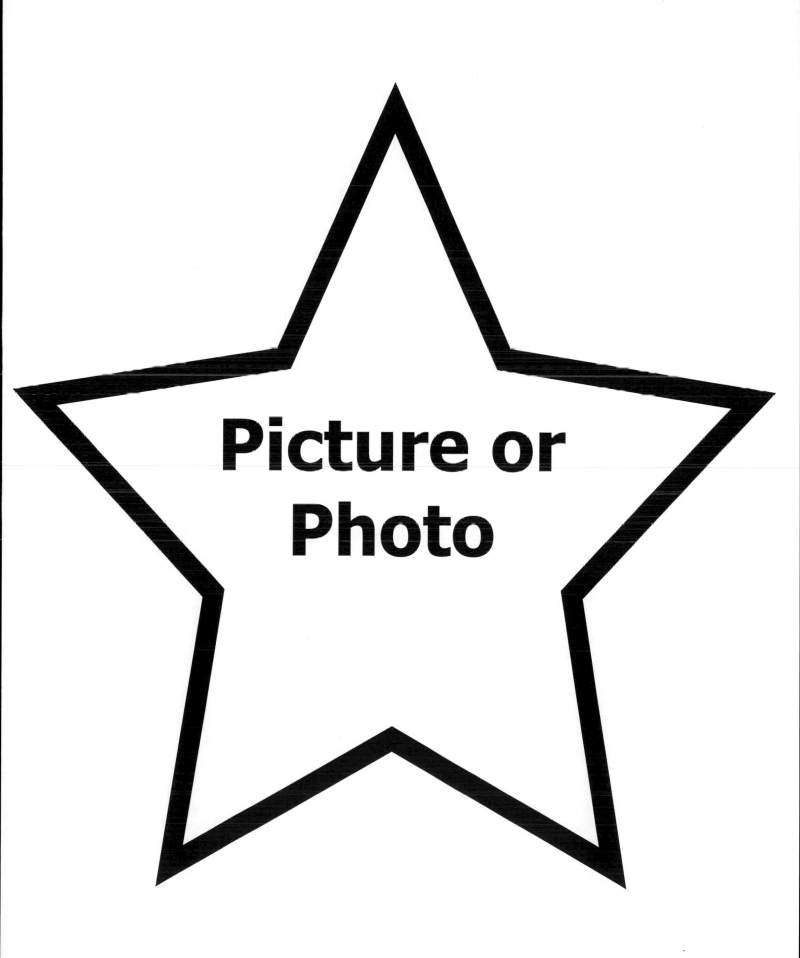

Picture or Photo

Biography
Walk of
Fame

Biography Review

Family

Job

Why Famous

Name

Other

Birth

Death

Life Experiences

S T A R   S E A R C H

1. What is your real name? Do you have any nicknames?

_____

_____

2. Where and when were you born?

_____

3. How old are you? _____

4. Can you tell me who is in your family? Which family member are you the closest to?

_____

_____

_____

5. What job would you like when you grow up? Why?

_____

_____

_____

6. Describe a memory that is exciting, fun, scary, terrifying, or sad so that we can learn more about you.

_____

_____

_____

7. What are your hobbies?

_____

_____

_____

8. What is your favorite part of school?

_____

_____

_____

9. What books do you like to read?

_____

_____

10. Is there anything else people should know about you?

_____

_____

Star

[Place photo here]

A Biography about _____

written by _____

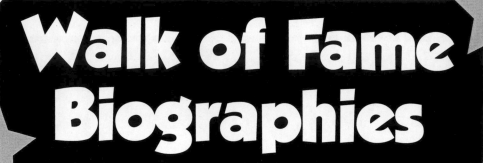

Walk of Fame Biographies

Book title

_____

Author

_____

This book is about _____

_____

_____

_____

_____

_____

_____

_____

I give this book _____ stars.

☆ ☆ ☆ ☆ ☆

(1=Okay, 5=Awesome)

Walk of Fame

Students at our school have been studying biographies during their visits to the library media center. After reading and evaluating several examples, the students interviewed classmates and wrote biographies of their peers. Take a stroll down our "Walk of Fame" to read about the celebrities at our school!

Chapter 8

Amazing Animals

Folktales

Let students' imaginations run wild with these lessons in folktales and folktale writing!

Grade Level: 4–5

Chapter Materials:

The following materials will be needed for each lesson in the chapter:

- Elements of folktales posters (pages 108–109)
- Colored copy paper or cardstock
- Laminating machine

Chapter Preparation:

1. Copy the elements of folktales posters.

2. Laminate and cut out the posters. Set aside for use in class. After lesson, hang in a central location for students to refer to throughout the unit.

Lesson 1: Amazing Animals

Time Required: 1 class period

Standards

1.1.5 Evaluate information found in selected sources on the basis of accuracy, validity, appropriateness for needs, importance, and social and cultural context.

1.1.6 Read, view, and listen for information presented in any format (e.g., textual, visual, media, digital) in order to make inferences and gather meaning.

1.4.3 Monitor gathered information, and assess for gaps or weaknesses.

Lesson Objectives

1. Students will correctly identify elements of the folktale genre.

2. Students will listen to a reading of an age-appropriate folktale and correctly recall elements of a folktale included in the book.

Additional Materials

- Folktale Bookmarks (page 110)
- Folktales about animal adaptations, such as:
  - *Why Mosquitoes Buzz in People's Ears* by Verna Aardema
  - *The Lizard and the Sun* by Alma Flor Ada
  - *How Rabbit Lost His Tale: a Traditional Cherokee Legend* by Deborah L. Duvall

- *How Many Spots Does a Leopard Have?: and Other Tales* by Julius Lester

- *How & Why Stories: World Tales Kids Can Read & Tell* by Martha Hamilton and Mitch Weiss

Lesson Preparation

1. Copy the Folktales Bookmarks onto card-stock or colored copy paper. Cut apart.

2. Pull examples of folktales that explain animal adaptations. Create a display in the 398.2 shelves of the nonfiction section. Set aside one to two stories to read aloud in class.

Lesson Plan

1. Gather students in the nonfiction section of the library media center.

2. Explain that they are going to study the folktale genre. Ask students if they know what folktales are and give students time to recall prior knowledge.

3. Show students the folktale examples on display in the nonfiction section. Booktalk the materials to pique students' interest. Explain that folktales are found in the nonfiction section under the Dewey Decimal number 398.2. Tell the students that they can find folktales at this location in any library that they visit.

4. Using the posters created from the repro-ducible section, explain to students what folktales are and common elements in-cluded in the genre. Tell students that they will study a specific type of folktale called a pourquoi story. These stories are used by different cultures to explain why some-thing, usually in nature, occurs.

5. Read and discuss age-appropriate folktales about animal adaptations.

6. Review with students what constitutes a folktale, common elements of folktales, and how the books read in class includes those elements.

7. Hang posters in an area where they may be referred to throughout the unit.

Lesson 2: Animal Research

Time Required: 2 class periods

Standards

1.1.4   Find, evaluate, and select appropriate sources to answer questions.

1.1.5   Evaluate information found in selected sources on the basis of accuracy, valid-ity, appropriateness for needs, impor-tance, and social and cultural context.

1.3.3   Follow ethical and legal guidelines in gathering and using information.

1.4.1   Monitor own information-seeking pro-cesses for effectiveness and progress, and adapt as necessary.

1.4.4   Seek appropriate help when it is needed.

Lesson Objectives

1. Students will correctly utilize encyclopedias and other reference resources to locate information on a topic.

2. Students will identify and record facts about a topic in their own words.

3. Students will adhere to ethical guidelines regarding the use of information, including rules of copyright and citation.

Additional Materials

- Research Worksheet (page 111)
- Animals for Folktales (page 114)
- Encyclopedias
- Nonfiction books and other resources about animals
- Computers with internet access
- Plastic bowl

Lesson Preparation

1. Copy the research worksheet (one per stu-dent).

2. Copy the Animals for Folktales list. Cut the list apart and place slips in plastic bowl.

3. Pull nonfiction books about the animals found on the list in the reproducible section and set aside for students to utilize in class.

Lesson Plan

1. Gather students in the nonfiction section of the library media center.

2. Ask students to recall what they remember about folktales from the previous lesson. Give students time to answer.

3. Review elements of folktales by utilizing the posters from the previous lesson. Also review the example folktales about animal adaptations read in previous lesson.

4. Explain to students that they are going to write their own pourquoi stories about animal adaptations. For example, one student might write a short story about how a tiger got its stripes while another could write a story about a dalmatian and its spots.

5. In order to write a folktale, they will first select an animal to learn more about. Then, they will research that animal to find out facts about its adaptation, habitat, food, enemies, and other defining factors.

6. Review how to utilize the encyclopedias and online search engines. Also, review the guidelines for selecting information to record, how to put that information into their own words, and information that must be recorded for citation purposes.

7. Show students the nonfiction resources pulled for their use in class. Also show students the 500 and 600 sections of the nonfiction shelves and remind them that information about animals is filed under these sections of the Dewey Decimal system.

8. Give each student a research worksheet.

9. Have students draw an animal from the plastic bowl and record the name of the animal on their research worksheet.

10. Give students remaining time to research their animal.

    (Note: This may require an additional class session.)

11. Collect research for use in next lesson.

Lesson 3: Animal Adaptations

Time Required: 2 class periods

Standards

2.1.1 Continue an inquiry-based research process by applying critical-thinking skills (analysis, synthesis, evaluation, organization) to information and knowledge in order to construct new understandings, draw conclusions, and create new knowledge.

2.1.2 Organize knowledge so that it is useful.

2.4.1 Determine how to act on information (accept, reject, modify).

Lesson Objectives

1. Students will correctly utilize pre-writing strategies to organize thoughts and ideas for a short story.

2. Students will select information from previous research to utilize in a completed writing product.

3. Students will adhere to ethical guidelines regarding the use of information, including rules of copyright and citation.

Additional Materials

- Research from previous lesson
- Storyboard Worksheet (page 112)
- Highlighters (one per student)
- Student example of research from previous lesson
- Overhead projector

Preparation

1. Copy the Storyboard Worksheet (one per student).

2. Copy an example of student research onto a transparency sheet.

Lesson Plan

1. Gather students in the nonfiction section of the library media center.

2. Ask students to recall what they remember about folktales from the previous lesson. Give students time to answer.

3. Review elements of folktales by utilizing the posters from the previous lesson.

4. Explain to students that they are going to begin writing their own pourquoi stories about animal adaptations. Tell them that before writing, most authors review their research and select information that they feel must be included in their written product. Explain that authors also reject information that they decide is not relevant to their report or story, or that they feel is inaccurate.

5. Place the example of student research on the overhead projector. Read the information aloud with the students. Using the students' input, demonstrate for them which information should be included in the story, and which information is not relevant for use. Highlight the information that should be included in the story.

6. Give each student their research and a highlighter. Have students highlight the information they feel is most important to their story and to explaining the animal's adaptations.

7. As students finish selecting information, give them a Storyboard worksheet. Have students complete the worksheet to plan the characters, plot, and resolution of their story.

   (Note: This may require an additional class session.)

8. Collect research and pre-writing worksheets for use in next lesson.

Lesson 4: Folktale Authors

Time Required: 2 class periods

Standards

2.1.2 Organize knowledge so that it is useful.

2.2.5 Demonstrate personal productivity by completing products to express learning.

3.1.4 Use writing and speaking skills to communicate new understandings effectively.

3.4.2 Assess the quality and effectiveness of the learning product.

Lesson Objectives

1. Students will utilize elements of a folktale to write a folktale about an animal adaptation.

2. Students will organize information in a logical manner.

3. Students will write to create a finished folktale to share with classmates.

Additional Materials

- Research and Storyboard worksheets from previous lessons

- Folktale worksheet (page 113)

Lersson Preparation

- Copy the Folktale Story worksheet (one per student).

Lesson Plan

1. Gather students in the nonfiction section of the library media center.

2. Ask students to recall what they remember about folktales from the previous lesson. Give students time to answer.

3. Review elements of folktales by utilizing the posters from the previous lesson.

4. Pass back students' research and Storyboard worksheets from previous lessons.

5. Explain that they will utilize the information from their research and pre-writing exercises to write a pourquoi story about how their animal got its adaptation.

6. Review writing ideas with students:

   a. They do not have to include every piece of information they found. Instead, they should utilize the information that they previously highlighted

   b. They should utilize each element of a folktale while writing.

   c. The information should be arranged in logical format, such as chronological order.

7. Give each student a folktale worksheet.

8. Give students class time to write their folktales. As they write, confer with them on their progress.

   (Note: This may require an additional class session.)

9. Collect folktales for use in next lesson.

Lesson 5: Author's Chair

Time Required: 1 class period

Standards

3.1.5 Use writing and speaking skills to communicate new understandings effectively.

3.2.3 Demonstrate leadership and confidence by presenting ideas to others in both formal and informal situations.

3.2.2 Show social responsibility by participating actively with others in learning situations and by contributing questions and ideas during group discussions.

Lesson Objectives

1. Students will share folktales by reading them to the class.

2. Students will demonstrate respect for classmates by being active, attentive listeners during sharing of folktales.

Additional Materials

- folktales from previous lesson
- leopard print material
- stool or chair

Lesson Preparation

- Set stool or chair at the head of the reading area. Drape with leopard print material.

Lesson Plan

1. Explain to students that this is the day they get to share their folktales with their classmates! Say, "Today, we are going to celebrate with our author's chair!"

2. Pass back folktales from previous lesson to the authors.

3. Gather students in the reading area.

4. Review expected behaviors for being active, attentive listeners.

5. Have students read their folktale to the class.

6. Hang folktales in the 398.2 section of the nonfiction shelves for others to read.

Folktale Rubric

CATEGORY	4	3	2	1
Research	All facts presented in the story are accurate.	Almost all facts presented in the story are accurate.	Most facts presented in the story are accurate	There are several factual errors in the story.
Organization	The story is very well organized.	The story is pretty well organized.	The story is a little hard to follow.	Ideas seem to be randomly arranged.
Spelling and Punctuation	There are no spelling or punctuation errors in the final draft.	There is one spelling or punctuation error in the final draft.	There are 2-3 spelling and punctuation errors in the final draft.	The final draft has more than 3 spelling and punctuation errors.
Solution/Resolution	The solution to the animal's adaptation is easy to understand.	The solution to the animal's adaptation is easy to understand and is somewhat logical.	The solution to the animal's adaptation is a little hard to understand.	No solution is attempted or it is impossible to understand the animal's adaptation.

Extension Idea

Provide students with material, felt, yarn, glitter, paper plates, popsicle sticks, and other craft items. Allow students to make a mask of their animal. Have students dramatize stories or utilize masks while reading their stories to their classmates.

Folktales

Passed on in oral tradition instead of being written down

Animals act like people

Typically include magic

Teach the reader a lesson

Setting is a far off time and place

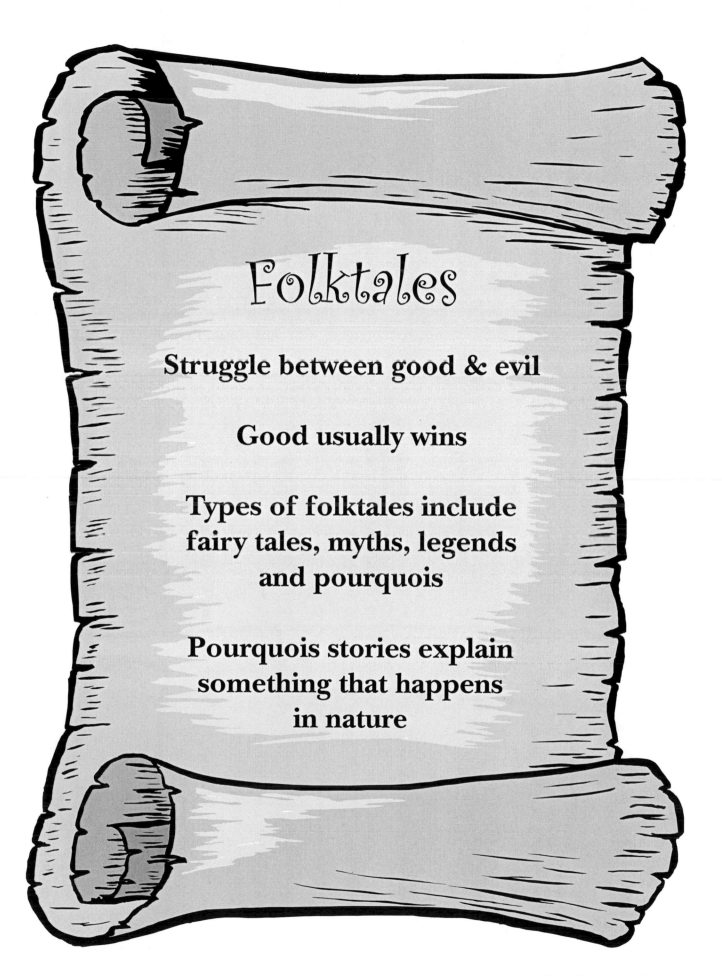

Folktales

Struggle between good & evil

Good usually wins

Types of folktales include
fairy tales, myths, legends
and pourquois

Pourquois stories explain
something that happens
in nature

Folktales Bookmarks

Folktales

* Passed on in oral tradition instead of being written down
* Animals act like people
* Typically include magic
* Teach the reader a lesson
* Setting is a far off time and place
* Struggle between good and evil
* Good usually wins
* Types of folktales include fairy tales, myths, and legends
* Try to explain something that happens in nature

Folktales

* Passed on in oral tradition instead of being written down
* Animals act like people
* Typically include magic
* Teach the reader a lesson
* Setting is a far off time and place
* Struggle between good and evil
* Good usually wins
* Types of folktales include fairy tales, myths, and legends
* Try to explain something that happens in nature

Folktales

* Passed on in oral tradition instead of being written down
* Animals act like people
* Typically include magic
* Teach the reader a lesson
* Setting is a far off time and place
* Struggle between good and evil
* Good usually wins
* Types of folktales include fairy tales, myths, and legends
* Try to explain something that happens in nature

Folktale Research

Animal: _____

Description	Habitat
Foods	Enemies
Behaviors	Other

Folktale Storyboard

Characters: _____

Setting: _____

Problem: _____

A Folktale by _____

Animals for Folktales

Animal	Adaptation
Tiger	Stripes
Leopard	Spots
Zebra	Stripes
Dalmatian	Spots
Rattlesnake	Rattle
Monkey	Long tail
Turtle	Shell
Elephant	Trunk
Porcupine	Quills
Chameleon	Changing colors
Deer	Antlers
Bat	Echolocation
Cheetah	Speed
Polar Bear	White fur
Giraffes	Long neck
Camel	Hump
Kangaroo	Pouch
Spider	Eight legs
Rabbit	Long ears
Lion	Mane
Pig	Snout
Skunk	Stripe
Squirrel	Bushy tail
Crocodile	Teeth
Alligator	Scaly skin

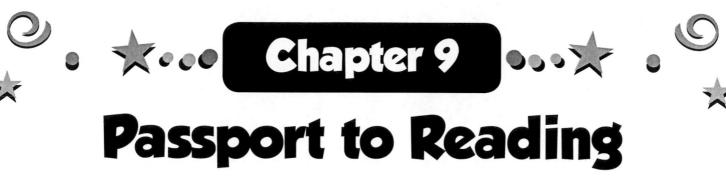

Chapter 9

Passport to Reading

Genre Study

Give students a passport to the world–via your library–with the genre-spanning lessons in this chapter.

Grade Level: 2–4

Chapter Materials: Time Required: 1 class period

Chapter Materials:

The following materials will be needed for each lesson in the chapter:

- Genre posters (pages 122–133)
- Laminating machine
- Books for each genre, suggestions include:

Fantasy

The Cat in the Hat by Dr. Seuss

Imogene's Antlers by David Small

Where the Wild Things Are by Maurice Sendak

Realistic fiction

Alexander and the Terrible, Horrible, No Good, Very Bad Day by Judith Viorst

Junie B., First Grader (at last!) by Barbara Park

When Sophie Gets Angry—Really, Really Angry by Molly Bang

Mystery

The Berenstain Bears and the Missing Dinosaur Bone by Jan and Stan Berenstain

Detective LaRue: Letters from the Investigation by Mark Teague

Encyclopedia Brown Gets His Man by Donald J. Sobel

Historical fiction

The Drinking Gourd by F. N. Monjo

John, Paul, George, and Ben by Lane Smith

Pink and Say by Patricia Polacco

Science Fiction

Hedgie Blasts Off! by Jan Brett

June 29, 1999 by David Wiesner

Ricky Ricotta's Giant Robot by Dav Pilkey

Biography

Martin's Big Words: the Life of Martin Luther King, Jr. by Doreen Rappaport

My Great-Aunt Arizona by Gloria Houston

Snowflake Bentley by Jacqueline Briggs Martin

Autobiography

Kickoff by Tiki Barber

The Wall: My Life Growing Up Behind the Red Curtain by Peter Sis

Knots in My Yo-Yo String by Jerry Spinelli

Poetry

Where the Sidewalk Ends by Shel Silverstein

Joyful Noise: Poems for Two Voices by Paul Fleischman

You Read to Me, I'll Read to You series by Mary Ann Hoberman

Fairy tales

Little Red Riding Hood by Trina Schart Hyman

Mufaro's Beautiful Daughters by John Steptoe

Rapunzel by Paul O. Zelinsky

Fables

Fables by Arnold Lobel

Once a Mouse by Marcia Brown

The Tortoise and the Hare by Janet Stevens

Legends

The Legend of the Bluebonnet by Tomie DePaola

The Legend of the Indian Paintbrush by Tomie DePaola

Saint George and the Dragon by Margaret Hodges

Tall tales

The Bunyans by Audrey Wood

The Gum Chewing Rattler by Joe Hayes

Johnny Appleseed by Steven Kellog

Chapter Preparation:

1. Copy and laminate the genre posters.

Lesson 1

Standards

1.1.2 Use prior and background knowledge as context for new learning.

2.1.2 Organize knowledge so that it is useful.

4.1.1 Read, view, and listen for pleasure and personal growth

Lesson Objectives

1. Students will correctly identify characteristics of specified genres.

2. Students will respond by recording facts and impressions learned through the reading of different genres.

Additional Materials

- Passport Cover Page (page 119)
- Passport Entry Pages (page 120)
- Passport End Page (page 121)
- Construction paper
- Stapler

Preparation

1. Copy the passport pages front to back so that the copies are double-sided. There should be one passport page per genre that you review (one copy per student).

2. Cut the construction paper to 8 ½" x 11" (one sheet per student).

Lesson Plan

1. Explain to students that you think reading and books can take people anywhere in the world. All you need is a good book and a great imagination and you can try anything you want! In fact, the entire class is going to use books to be globetrotters! Explain that globetrotters are people who like to travel and go places.

2. Explain to students that they are going to be Genre Globetrotters. The library media center is full of wonderful books and you've noticed that some students always read the same types of books. So, you want them to "travel" to other parts of the library and try new books!

3. Write the word "genre" on the board and explain that "genre" refers to a type of book. All of the books in a genre are similar and share certain characteristics. During this unit, the students will read books of different genres and have an opportunity to see other books that share the same characteristics.

4. Tell students that globetrotters usually have a passport that allows them to visit other countries. It also shows a record of the places they have visited. Explain that they are going to make Book Passports to make a record of all the wonderful books that they read during this unit.

5. Give each student a copy of the passport pages. Have them fold passport pages in half.

6. Give each student a piece of construction paper. Have them fold the construction paper around their passport pages to form a cover. Staple all the passports together. If time allows, let students decorate their passport covers.

7. Introduce the genre of the week by using the poster to explain the characteristics to the students.

8. Booktalk several titles for that genre and show the covers to the students.

9. Read an example of the genre aloud to students.

10. Discuss the book and how it fulfills the criteria of that genre.

11. Have students fill out a page in their Book Passport for that genre and book example. Ask students to write down a fact about that genre and not just information about the book on the passport page.

12. Collect Book Passports for use in next lesson.

Repeat this lesson each week in the unit until you have reviewed all genres that you wish with the students. The next lesson is the culminating activity.

Lesson 2: My Bag Is Packed: I'm Ready to Read !

Standards

1.1.2 Use prior and background knowledge as context for new learning.

2.1.2 Organize knowledge so that it is useful.

4.1.1 Read, view, and listen for pleasure and personal growth.

Lesson Objectives

1. Students will correctly identify characteristics of specified genres.

2. Students will respond by recording facts and impressions learned through the reading of different genres.

Additional Materials

- Suitcase Worksheet (page 134)
- brown construction paper
- scissors

Preparation

1. Copy the suitcase worksheet onto brown construction paper (one copy per student).

Lesson Plan

1. Tell students now that they have been Genre Globetrotters, you want to hear about the favorite book that they visited. Explain to students that when globetrotters return home from their travels, they like to show their friends pictures and souvenirs of their adventures. Today, they are going to create a display of their favorite genre.

2. Give each student a copy of the suitcase and a pair of scissors. Have students cut out their suitcase.

3. Tell students that you want them to fill in the information on their suitcase. Then, you want them to draw pictures on their suitcase that depict their favorite genre.

4. Give students time to complete their suitcase.

5. Collect suitcases. Hang on bulletin board with the sign "Genre Globetrotters: Reading is Our Passport to Great Books!"

Genre Suitcase Rubric

CATEGORY	4	3	2	1
Illustrations	Illustrations are neat, recognizable, and depict the genre.	Illustrations are mainly neat, recognizable, and depict the genre.	Illustrations are neat or recognizable, but do not depict the genre.	Illustrations are not neat or recognizable, and do not depict the genre.
Genre	Suitcase includes many facts about the specified genre.	Suitcase includes some facts about the specified genre.	Suitcase includes few facts about the specified genre.	Suitcase includes no facts about the specified genre.
Attractiveness	The worksheet is exceptionally attractive.	The worksheet is somewhat attractive.	The worksheet is a little messy.	The worksheet is very messy.

Extension Idea

Copy the postcard template on page 135 onto cardstock. Have students fill out the postcard about a genre they read about in class and draw a picture of a book that is an example of that genre on the front of the postcard. Ask students to "mail" the postcards to their friends and have them try new books from the library media center.

Passport Cover Page

Reading is your passport to the world !

This passport belongs to

Citizen of the Library

Reading is your passport to the world !

This passport belongs to

Citizen of the Library

Passport Entry Page

Date:
Genre:
Author:
Title:

Something I learned about this genre:

My favorite part of the book was:

Date:
Genre:
Author:
Title:

Something I learned about this genre:

My favorite part of the book was:

Passport End Page

Date:

Genre:

Author:

Title:

Something I learned about this genre:

My favorite part of the book was:

Tell which book is your favorite and explain why.

Fantasy

Make-believe stories that contain elements that are not real. For example, they might have talking animals or magic.

Realistic Fiction

Make-believe stories that contain events and people that could really happen. They take place in this time.

Mystery

Make-believe stories that contain crimes or puzzles that are not solved until the end of the stories.
They keep readers in suspense.

Historical Fiction

Make-believe stories that take place in a time period in the past. The setting is real but the characters are fictional.

Science Fiction

Make-believe stories that contain science and technology, like robots, computers, etc.

Biography

True stories about real people's lives. They are written by someone other than the people they are about.

Autobiography

True stories about real people's lives. They are written by the people that they are about.

Poetry

Written in verse in a way that makes the reader feel emotions.
Sometimes includes rhyme and rhythm.

Fairy Tales

Make-believe stories about heroic deeds that include folk characters. They typically include magic and happy endings.

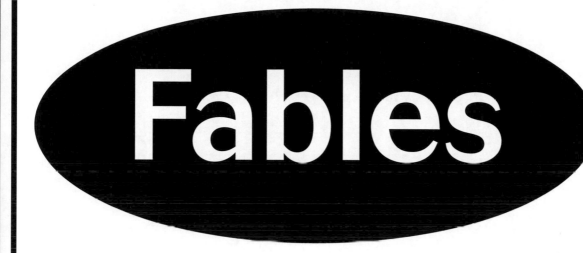

Fables

Short stories that try to teach
the reader a lesson. Usually, they
have animal characters that talk
and act like humans.

Legends

Stories about historical events
or real people that contain a
mix of fiction and facts.

Tall Tales

Make-believe stories in which the main character is "larger than life."

Globetrotter's Name:

My favorite genre is _____

Books in my favorite genre are about _____

A great book in my favorite genre is _____

Why is my book a good example of this genre? _____

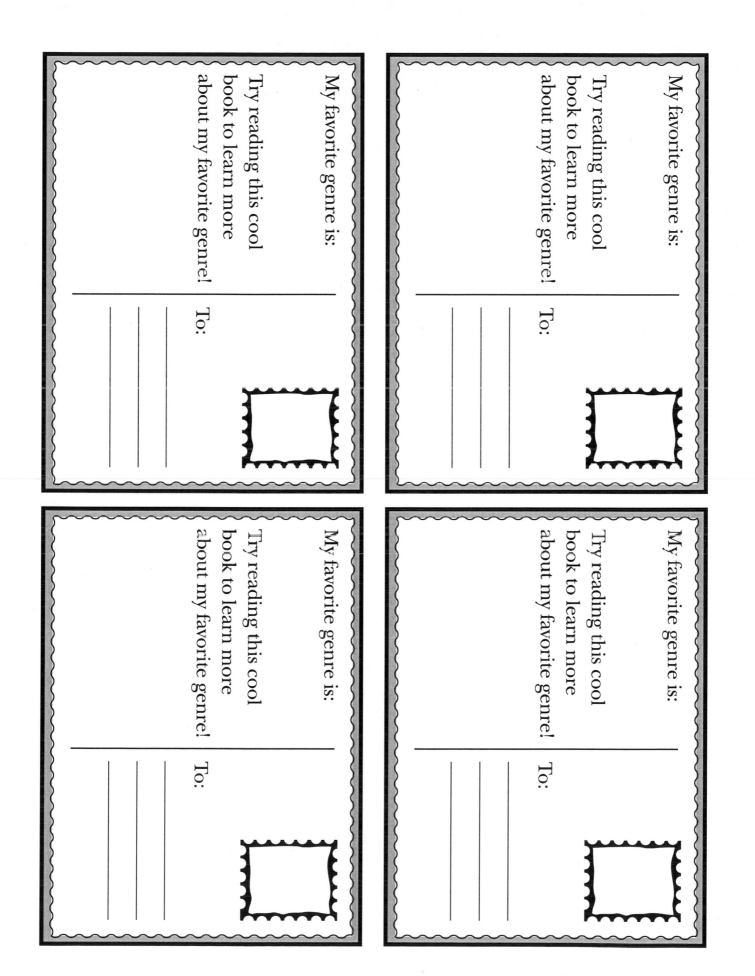

My favorite genre is:

Try reading this cool
book to learn more
about my favorite genre!

To:

My favorite genre is:

Try reading this cool
book to learn more
about my favorite genre!

To:

My favorite genre is:

Try reading this cool
book to learn more
about my favorite genre!

To:

My favorite genre is:

Try reading this cool
book to learn more
about my favorite genre!

To:

Chapter 10

Best Seller List

Book Reviews

Introduce students to the art of the book review in these lessons. By the time they are finished, they'll be writing reviews, themselves!

Grade Level: 2–5

Lesson 1: Book Brainstorm

Standards

1.1.2 Use prior and background knowledge as context for new learning.

2.1.2 Organize knowledge so that it is useful.

2.1.1 Read, view, and listen for pleasure and personal growth.

2.4.2 Identify own areas of interest.

Lesson Objectives

1. Students will identify elements of a book review.

2. Students will identify one or more works of literature read on an individual basis for aesthetic purposes.

3. Students will correctly utilize pre-writing strategies to organize ideas for a written book review.

Materials

- A copy of a bestseller list (such as *The New York Times Best Seller List*)

- Examples of written book reviews from a newspaper, magazine, etc.

- Book Review Checklist (page 139)

- Transparencies

- Overhead projector

- Dry erase board and marker

Preparation

1. Copy the bestseller's list and written book reviews onto transparencies.

2. Set up overhead projector and screen.

3. Copy the book review checklist. (one per student)

Lesson Plan

1. Place the transparency of the bestseller list on the overhead projector for all students to see. Explain to students what a bestseller list is. Typically, these lists that show books with the highest sales for the week. It lets people know which books are considered popular. Some readers use these lists to determine what they will read next.

2. Place the transparency of the first book review on the overhead projector for all students to see. Explain to students that a book review tries to "sell" a book to an audience. Typically, it gives them just enough information to hook their interest and make them want to read the book. It also explains why the reviewer likes or dislikes the book. Read the book reviews to the students to show them several examples of book reviews.

3. Ask students to name things that they saw in each book review. For example, each book review might have included the title of the book or special features that the book contained.

4. Give students time to brainstorm and record their answers on the dry erase board.

5. After allowing the students to brainstorm a list of elements of a book review, make sure that these items are all included on the list:

   a. Reviewer's name

   b. Title of book

   c. Author and illustrator's names

   d. Main character

   e. Problem/conflict

   f. Something interesting about the book

   g. How the reviewer feels about the book

6. Explain to students that they are going to use these things to write a book review of their favorite book. They will be selling books to other students in the school!

7. Give each student a book review checklist.

8. Give students remaining time in class to complete checklist.

9. Collect checklists for use in next lesson.

Lesson 2: Two Thumbs Up

Standards

1.1.3 Use prior and background knowledge as context for new learning.

2.1.3 Organize knowledge so that it is useful.

3.1.3 Use writing and speaking skills to communicate new understandings effectively.

Lesson Objectives

1. Students will utilize organized information to create a written product.

2. Students will write a book review for a work of literature read on an individual basis for aesthetic purposes.

Materials

- Book review checklists from previous lesson

- Book Review Template (page 140)

- Examples of written book reviews from a newspaper, magazine, etc.

Preparation

- Copy the book review template (one per student).

Lesson Plan

1. Ask students to recall what they remember about book reviews from the previous lesson. Give students time to answer.

2. Review elements of a book review with students.

3. Pass back book review checklists from previous lesson.

4. Explain to students that today, they will use the information they organized on the checklist to write their book review.

5. Reread the example book reviews aloud to students. Remind them that they are "selling" the book to other students. Their writing should be creative and informational without giving away the ending of the book.

6. Give each student a copy of the book review template.

7. Give students remaining time in class to write their book review.

8. Collect book reviews for next lesson.

Lesson 3: Critic's Corner

Standards

3.1.3 Use writing and speaking skills to communicate new understandings effectively.

3.2.1 Demonstrate leadership and confidence by presenting ideas to others in both formal and informal situations.

3.3.5 Contribute to the exchange of ideas within and beyond the learning community.

Lesson Objectives

1. Students will share written book reviews by reading them to the class.

2. Students will demonstrate respect for classmates by being active, attentive listeners during sharing of book reviews.

Materials

- Book reviews from previous lesson

- Posterboard

- Markers
- Stool or chair

Preparation

1. Using a marker, write [class name] Best Seller List at the top of the posterboard.

2. Set stool or chair at the head of the reading area.

Lesson Plan

1. Explain to students that this is the day they will get to be critics. They will read their book reviews aloud to their classmates.

2. Pass back book reviews from previous lesson to the students.

3. Gather students in the reading area.

4. Review expected behaviors for being active, attentive listeners.

5. Have students read their book review to the class.

6. After a student reads his or her book review, have him or her write the title of their book on the posterboard.

7. After class, hang the posterboard in the hallway. Surround the posterboard with the students' book reviews.

Book Review Rubric

CATEGORY	4	3	2	1
Required Elements	The book review contains all of the listed requirements for a book review	The book review contains most of the listed requirements for a book review.	The book review contains few of the listed requirements for a book review.	The book review contains none of the listed requirements for a book review.
Description	The book review described the book in an interesting way without revealing the ending.	The book review described the book in a somewhat interesting way without revealing the ending.	The book review briefly described the book and/or revealed the ending.	The book review did not accurately describe the book and/or revealed the ending.
Hook	The book review uses a hook to entice the listener to read the book.	The book review uses a hook to entice the listener to read the book.	The book review does not use a hook to entice the listener to read the book.	The book review does not use a hook to entice the listener to read the book.
Organization	The information in the book review was organized logically.	The information in the book review was organized somewhat logically.	The information in the book review was somewhat organized but jumped around.	The information in the book review was not organized.

Extension Idea

Locate an episode of *Reading Rainbow*. Cue tape to the book reviews and show to students. As students read their book reviews, videotape them. Include these book reviews on the school news program. Or, have students read their book reviews as an announcement each morning to encourage other students to read those books.

Book Review Checklist

☐ **Your name**

_____

☐ **Title of the book**

_____

☐ **Author and illustrator's names**

Written by _____

Illustrated by _____

☐ **Who is the main character?**

_____

☐ **What is the problem in this book?**

_____
_____
_____
_____

☐ **What is the most interesting or exciting thing in this book?**

_____
_____
_____

☐ **How did you feel about this book?**

_____
_____

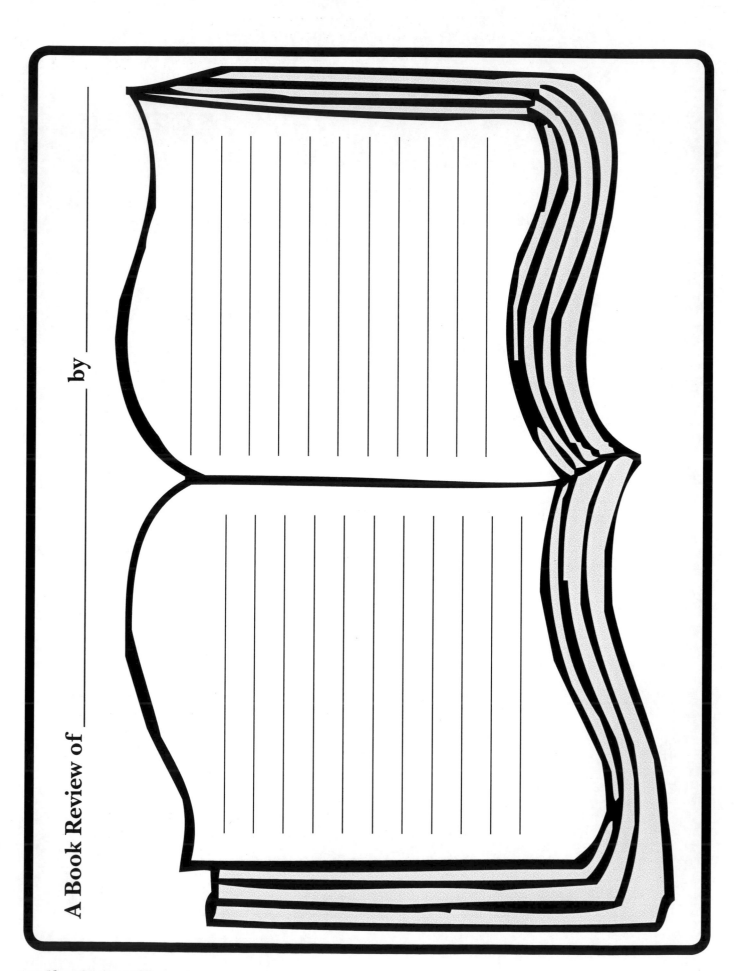

A Book Review of _____

by _____

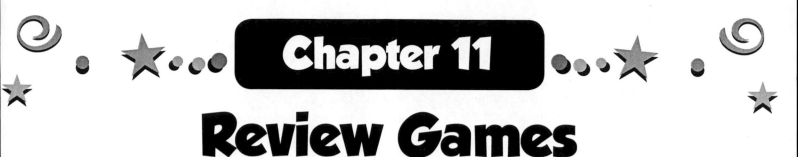

Chapter 11

Review Games

Games and trivia to grow students' confidence and reinforce their knowledge of the library media center

Grade Level: 4–5

Game 1: Library Hangman

Standards

1.1.3 Develop and refine a range of questions to frame the search for new understanding.

1.1.9 Collaborate with others to broaden and deepen understanding.

Objectives

1. Students will correctly identify library media center resources utilized during the research process.

2. Students will correctly identify library and information literacy skills utilized for access and retrieval of information.

3. Students will correctly demonstrate good sportsmanship conduct and teamwork.

Materials

- Library Hangman worksheet (page 144)
- Question Sets (pages 145–148)
- Laminating machine
- Dry erase markers

Preparation

1. Copy hangman gallows reproduction (one set per four students).

2. Copy Question Sets (one copy per four students).

Or, develop your own questions (or have students develop questions) that cover topics taught in the library media center.

3. Laminate Question Sets and Library Hangman worksheet for durability and reuse through play.

Procedures

1. Divide students into groups of four. In that group of four, partner students to form Team A and Team B.

2. Provide each group of four with a Library Hangman worksheet and a dry erase marker.

3. Provide a question set to each team. Team A will receive Question Set A while Team B will receive Question Set B.

4. Team A challenges Team B first by asking them the first question on their Team A Question Set. If Team B correctly answers the question, Team A continues with the next question. If Team B answers incorrectly, then Team A draws a part of a hangman on the laminated worksheet.

5. Play continues in this manner with the remaining questions from Team A's question set. If Team B forms a hangman before answering all questions for Team A, then they lose 5 points. If they answer all the questions before forming a hangman, they receive a bonus of 5 points.

6. At the end of Team A's questions or Team B forming a hangman (whichever occurs first), the worksheet is erased and the teams switch places.

7. Play continues as Team B challenges Team A with their Question Set and repeats steps 4-5 above.

8. At the end of this round, members of each team should receive new question sets in order to continue play.

9. After time is called, the Team with the highest number of points is declared the winner.

Game 2: Trivia Contest

Standards

1.1.4 Find, evaluate, and select appropriate sources to answer questions.

1.2.2 Demonstrate confidence and self-direction by making independent choices in the selection of resources and information.

1.4.1 Monitor own information-seeking processes for effectiveness and progress, and adapt as necessary.

Objectives

1. Students will correctly identify library media center resources utilized during the research process.

2. Students will correctly use library media center resources to locate the answer to a question related to the school curriculum.

3. Students will self-monitor their progress in locating information and adapt resources or search strategies as necessary.

Materials

- Trivia contest fliers (page 149)
- Trivia contest poster (page 150)
- Trivia questions
- Small box
- Basket
- Scratch paper

- Small prizes
- Laminating machine

Preparation

1. Copy the trivia contest fliers. Pass out one to every student.

2. Copy and laminate the trivia contest poster. Hang in a central area where all students in the building will be able to view the questions.

3. Ask teachers for questions that stem from their curriculum. Gather one question for each week of the school year. Ensure that questions are challenging enough that students must use library media center resources, such as the dictionary, encyclopedia, thesaurus, etc., to locate the answers.

4. Cut a hole in the top of the box so that students can drop their entries in it throughout the week.

5. Place the scratch paper in the basket next to the answer box.

Explanation

1. At the beginning of the week, post the current trivia question on the trivia poster in the designated section.

2. Give students the entire week to utilize library resources to locate answers.

3. Have students record their name and answer on a piece of scratch paper and drop it into the answer box.

4. At the end of the week, draw a paper from the box. Continue drawing until an entry with the correct answer is found.

5. Announce the winner over the intercom. Have winner visit the library to select a prize.

Game 3: Brain Sharpener

Standards

1.1.3 Develop and refine a range of questions to frame the search for new understanding.

1.1.9 Collaborate with others to broaden and deepen understanding.

Objectives

1. Students will correctly identify library media center resources utilized during the research process.

2. Students will correctly identify library and information literacy skills utilized for access and retrieval of information.

3. Students will correctly demonstrate good sportsmanship conduct and teamwork.

Materials

- Timer
- Small plastic bowl or container
- Pencils
- Pencil sharpeners
- Brain Sharpener game questions (pages 151–153)
- Laminating machine

Preparation

1. Copy game questions. Cut apart and laminate for durability. Or, develop your own questions or have students develop questions that cover topics taught in the library media center. Place questions in plastic bowl or container.

2. Purchase pencils and pencil sharpeners as prizes for the winners.

Explanation

1. Divide students into four groups.

2. Decide which team will play first.

3. Assign a member from the second team to be the timekeeper and a member of the third team to be the scorekeeper.

4. Have the timekeeper set the timer to two minutes.

5. Start the game when the timekeeper begins clocking the two minutes.

6. Pull questions out of the container and read them to the first team up for play. Any team member may answer the question with or without waiting for the entire question to be read. Play stays on the same question until the team answers correctly or elects to move to a new question. If the team does not know the answer to the question, they yell "Pass" and play continues with a new question. Continue reading questions until the two-minute playing time is over.

7. The team earns one point for each question answered correctly. One point is deducted for each time they "pass" on a question.

8. At the end of the first team's play, record their score on the board and move to the second team. Place all the questions back in the container. Explain to students that this is why it is important to pay attention as other groups play. They may get a repeat question and have the advantage of hearing the questions and answers several times.

9. Repeat steps 3-8 until each team has had the opportunity to play.

10. The group with the highest score wins! Each member of the group gets a pencil and pencil sharpener.

Extension Idea

Divide students into small groups. Explain to each group that they will create a board game for primary students. They must select one aspect of the library media center, such as book care, call numbers, beginning research, famous authors, etc., that the primary students learn about in the media center. Then, they will create a board game, complete with playing pieces, directions, and rules, to review that topic with the primary students.

LIBRARY HANGMAN

Library Hangman
Question Set IA

1. To find the meanings and spellings of words, what reference book would I use?

   Dictionary

2. How are fiction books shelved?

   Alphabetical order by author's last name

3. To find a synonym for a word, what reference book would I need?

   Thesaurus

4. To locate a geographical location, what reference book could I use?

   Atlas

5. What is the first step in the Big6 research model?

   Task definition

6. In the first step of the Big6 research model, what do you do?

   State the problem or question

7. To research someone's life, what type of book would I need?

   Biography

8. How are biographies shelved?

   Alphabetical order by the last name of the person they are about

9. What section of a book lists the subjects and chapters found in the book?

   Table of Contents

10. Books that are make-believe are called _____?

    Fiction

11. This resource includes informative articles, poetry, editorials, and other columns.

    Magazine or periodical

12. The second step of the Big 6 research model is called _____?

    Information seeking strategy

13. A resource that contains news, features, opinions, and advertising is a _____?

    Newspaper

14. What do we call the list of resources used in writing a paper or book?

    Bibliography

15. What is a list of words with definitions located in the back of a book called?

    Glossary

1. What reference source is used to research people, places, and things?

   Encyclopedia

2. How are nonfiction books shelved?

   By Dewey Decimal number

3. How are encyclopedias arranged?

   In alphabetical order by topic

4. To research a person in an encyclopedia, would I look up their first or last name?

   Last name

5. If I copy my report straight from a reference source, it is called _____.

   Plagiarism

6. What computer program is used to locate which books the library owns?

   Card Catalog or OPAC

7. What is the date a book is published?

   Copyright date

8. What is a book about a person's life written by that person?

   Autobiography

9. What are true or informational books called?

   Nonfiction

10. What is the third step of the Big6 research model?

    Location and access

11. In the third step of the Big6 research model, what does a researcher do?

    Gather information

12. Books used for research that do not check out of the library are called _____.

    Reference

13. What page of the book tells us when and where the book was made?

    Copyright page

14. What is the fourth step of the Big6 research model?

    Use of information

15. What does a researcher do during the fourth step of the Big6 research model?

    Select which information to use

Library Hangman
Question Set 2A

1. What do we call the words at the top of encyclopedia and dictionary pages that tell us the first and last topics found on the page?

   Guide words

2. To look up a topic in the encyclopedia, what letter should I look under?

   The first letter in the topic's name

3. What is the fifth step of the Big6 research model?

   Synthesis

4. What does a researcher do during the fifth step of the Big6 research model?

   Organize the information and create a product

5. What topic is found in the 200 section of the Dewey Decimal system?

   Religion and mythology

6. Ina list of subjects found in the back of the book is called the _____.

   Index

7. What topic is found in the 300 section of the Dewey Decimal system?

   Fairy tales, legends, and holidays

8. Instead of copying research word for word, I should _____.

   Put it in my own words

9. When I give credit to the books and authors whose information I use, I am completing the _____ process.

   Citation

10. To look up Abraham Lincoln in the encyclopedia, I would look under which letter?

    L

11. To look up tigers in the encyclopedia, I would look under which letter?

    T

12. A reference book that provides lists of what happened in certain years is an _____.

    Almanac

13. What topic is found in the 600 section of the Dewey Decimal system?

    Applied science and technology

14. What topic is found in the 700 section of the Dewey Decimal system?

    Sports, music, arts, and other recreation

15. To look up the United States in the encyclopedia, I would look under which letter?

    U

1. What is the sixth step of the Big6 research model?

   Evaluation

2. What does a researcher do during the sixth step of the Big6 research model?

   Evaluate the research process and final product

3. What do we call a book's address in the library?

   Call number

4. What topic is found in the 000 section of the Dewey Decimal system?

   General knowledge

5. What topic is found in the 400 section of the Dewey Decimal system?

   Language

6. What topic is found in the 500 section of the Dewey Decimal system?

   Natural science

7. To look up George Washington in the encyclopedia, I would look under which letter?

   W

8. What topic is found in the 100 section of the Dewey Decimal system?

   Philosophy, feelings, and other things people think about

9. To look up Canada in the encyclopedia, I would look under which letter?

   C

10. A website that allows me to look for information is called a _____.

    Search engine

11. What topic is found in the 800 section of the Dewey Decimal system?

    Literature (plays, jokes, poetry)

12. To look up a red-tailed fox in the encyclopedia, I would look under which letter?

    F

13. What topic is found in the 900 section of the Dewey Decimal system?

    History and geography

14. Name an example of a search engine.

    Ask.com, Yahoo, Google, etc.

15. What do we call the date a book is due back at the library?

    Due date

Trivia Contest Fliers

Library Trivia Contest

Come stretch your brain with the library's weekly trivia contest! Each Monday, a new trivia question will be posted on the trivia contest bulletin board. Read the question and research the answer by Friday. Then, drop your full name and answer in the answer box on the library desk. Winners will be drawn each Friday

Library Trivia Contest

Come stretch your brain with the library's weekly trivia contest! Each Monday, a new trivia question will be posted on the trivia contest bulletin board. Read the question and research the answer by Friday. Then, drop your full name and answer in the answer box on the library desk. Winners will be drawn each Friday

Library Trivia Contest

Come stretch your brain with the library's weekly trivia contest! Each Monday, a new trivia question will be posted on the trivia contest bulletin board. Read the question and research the answer by Friday. Then, drop your full name and answer in the answer box on the library desk. Winners will be drawn each Friday

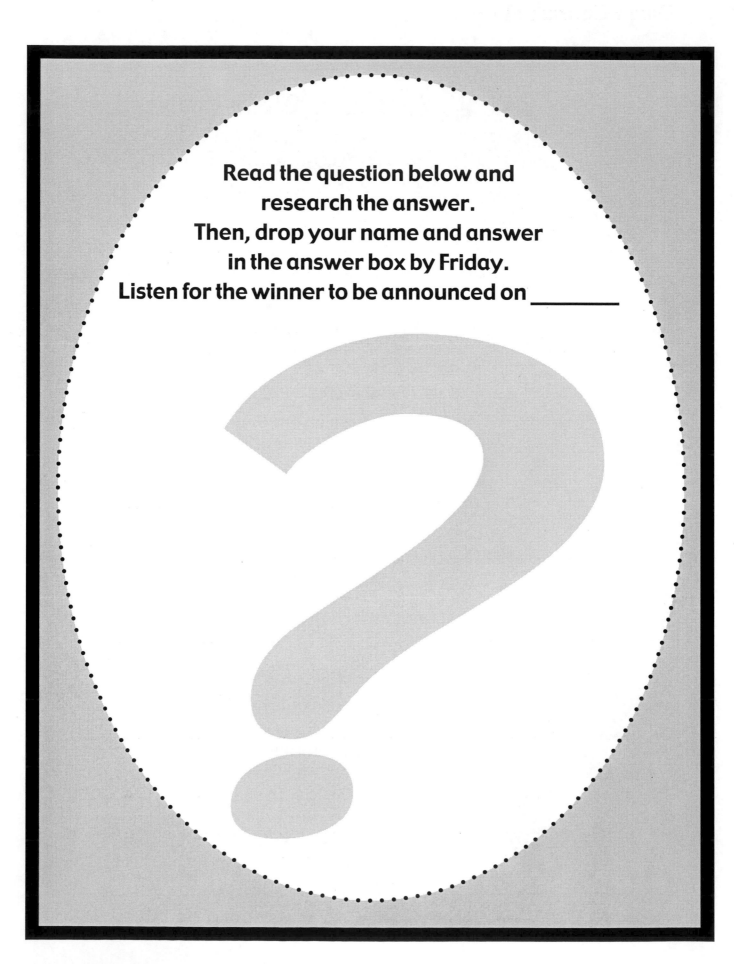

Read the question below and
research the answer.
Then, drop your name and answer
in the answer box by Friday.
Listen for the winner to be announced on _____

Game Questions

The Brain Sharpener

What is the name of the book that gives
the meanings of words?

Dictionary

The Brain Sharpener

What book allows us to research people,
places, and things?

Encyclopedia

The Brain Sharpener

Dictionaries and encyclopedias are
arranged in what order?

Alphabetical

The Brain Sharpener

Books about real things are called _____.

Nonfiction

The Brain Sharpener

Books that are make-believe are called _____.

Fiction

The Brain Sharpener

Nonfiction books are shelved in what order?

Dewey decimal system

The Brain Sharpener

Fiction books are shelved in what order?

Alphabetical by author's last name

The Brain Sharpener

Books about people's lives are called _____.

Biographies

The Brain Sharpener

Biographies are shelved in what order?

Alphabetical by the last name of the person they are about

Game Questions

The Brain Sharpener
What book gives us synonyms of words?
Thesaurus

The Brain Sharpener
A list of words with their meanings at the back of
a book is called a _____.
Glossary

The Brain Sharpener
A list of subjects found at the back of a book
is called an _____.
Index

The Brain Sharpener
A list of chapters and topics found at the beginning
of a book is called the _____.
Table of contents

The Brain Sharpener
A collection of maps is called an _____.
Atlas

The Brain Sharpener
Books that do not check out of
the library are _____.
Reference

The Brain Sharpener
This resource includes informative articles, poetry,
editorials, and other columns.
Magazine

The Brain Sharpener
A resource that provides daily news, editorials,
sports, and other features.
Newspaper

The Brain Sharpener
The date a book is published is the _____.
Copyright date

Game Questions

The Brain Sharpener

Copying someone else's work word for word is called _____.

Plagiarism

The Brain Sharpener

The computer program used to look up books in the library is the _____.

Card catalog or OPAC

The Brain Sharpener

An award given each year to the best illustrations in a children's book is called the _____.

Caldecott Medal

The Brain Sharpener

An award given each year to the best story in a children's book is called the _____.

Newbery Medal

The Brain Sharpener

The date your book is due back at the library.

Due date

The Brain Sharpener

The part of the book that holds the pages together.

Spine

The Brain Sharpener

The page that provides the title, author, and name of the publisher is the _____.

Title page

The Brain Sharpener

The company that prints the book is the _____.

Publisher

The Brain Sharpener

A book about a person's life written by that person is called an _____.

Autobiography

Resource Guide

The following is information on resources utilized throughout the units in this book. The resources are organized by the chapter in which they were referred.

Introduction

American Association of School Librarians
www.ala.org/ala/aasl/aaslindex.cfm

The Library Dragon by Carmen Agra Deedy and matching flip doll are available from Peachtree Publishers. The book is $16.95 and the flip doll is $28.95.

> Peachtree Publishers
> 1700 Chattahoochee Avenue
> Atlanta, GA 30318-2112
> Phone: 800-241-0113
> *http://peachtree-online.com/Default.aspx*

Magic wands may be purchased from Tree Blocks. They are available in 11 different shapes. I have found the star shaped to be the most effective. Each wand costs $6.50.

> Tree Blocks
> 1187 Coast Village Road, #112
> Santa Barbara, CA 93108
> Phone: 800-873-4960
> *www.treeblocks.com/music_wands.htm*

Standards for the 21st Century Learner are available for download from the American Association of School Librarians' website at http://www.ala.org/ala/aasl/aaslproftools/learningstandards/standards.cfm. The standards may also be ordered in packets of 12 for $13.50 for ALA members and $14.95 for non-members.

> American Library Association
> 50 E. Huron
> Chicago, IL 60611
> Phone: 800-545-2433
> *www.ala.org/ala/productsandpublications/products_and_publications.cfm*

Chapter 1

Luau decorations, such as leis, a hula skirt, and palm trees, are available for order from Oriental Trading. On their website, click on "Luau" to browse available items and decorations.

> Oriental Trading
> 4206 S. 108th Street
> Omaha NE 68136
> Phone: 800-875-8480
> *www.orientaltrading.com*

Chapter 2

The Incredible Book-Eating Boy by Oliver Jeffers is available from Penguin Group. The cost is $16.99.

> Penguin Group
> 375 Hudson Street
> New York, NY 10014
> Phone: 800-847-5515
> *http://us.penguingroup.com/*

The sticker paper referred to for these lessons is Avery Sticker Project Paper 3383. This paper is available at business supply stores.

The address labels referred to for these lessons are Avery Easy Peel White Address Labels 5160. The labels are available at business supply stores.

Chapter 3

Information on the Big6 and Super3 can be found at *www.big6.com, www.linworth.com,* and *www.upstartpromotions.com.* Big6 and Super3 poster sets are also available from Upstart Books. The Big6 elementary level poster set costs $14.95 and the Super3 poster set costs $9.95.

UpstartBooks
W5527 State Road 106
P.O. Box 800
Fort Atkinson, WI 53538-0800
Phone: 800-448-4887
www.highsmith.com

Chapter 5

Dewey Decimal posters are available from Upstart Books. The Dewey poster set costs $24.95.

UpstartBooks
W5527 State Road 106
P.O. Box 800
Fort Atkinson, WI 53538-0800
Phone: 800-448-4887
www.highsmith.com

Chapter 7

Wilma Unlimited by Kathleen Krull is available from Amazon. The cost is $29.95.

Amazon
www.amazon.com

Hollywood Walk of Fame
www.hollywoodchamber.net/icons/history.asp

Click on "Walk of Fame" on the right-hand side for photographs

Chapter 8

How & Why Stories: World Tales Kids Can Read & Tell by Martha Hamilton and Mitch Weiss is available from August House. The cost is $16.95.

August House
3500 Piedmont Road, NE
Suite 310
Atlanta, GA 30305
Phone: 800-284-8784
www.augusthouse.com/

How Many Spots Does a Leopard Have?: and Other Tales by Julius Lester is available from Scholastic. The cost is $6.95.

Scholastic Inc.
557 Broadwa
New York, NY 10012
Phone: 800-724-652-7842
www2.scholastic.com/browse/home.jsp

How Rabbit Lost His Tale: a Traditional Cherokee Legend by Deborah L. Duvall is available from the University of New Mexico Press. The cost is $14.95.

University of New Mexico Press
Order Department
1312 Basehart Rd. SE
Albuquerque, NM 87106-4363
Phone: 800-249-7737
www.unmpress.com/

The Lizard and the Sun by Alma Flor Ada is available from Random House. The cost is $6.99.

Random House
1745 Broadway
New York, NY 10019
Phone: 212-782-9000
www.randomhouse.com/

Why Mosquitoes Buzz in People's Ears by Verna Aardema is available from Penguin Group. The cost is $16.99.

Penguin Group
375 Hudson Street
New York, NY 10014
Phone: 800-847-5515
http://us.penguingroup.com/

Chapter 9

Alexander and the Terrible, Horrible, No Good, Very Bad Day by Judith Viorst is available from Simon & Schuster. The cost is $16.95.

Simon & Schuster
1230 Avenue of the Americas, 11th Fl.
New York, NY 10020
Phone: 212-698-700
www.simonsays.com

The Berenstain Bears and the Missing Dinosaur Bone by Jan and Stan Berenstain is available from Random House. The cost is $8.99.

Random House
1745 Broadway
New York, NY 10019
Phone: 212-782-900
www.randomhouse.com/

The Bunyans by Audrey Wood is available from Scholastic. The cost is $5.99.

Scholastic Inc.
557 Broadwa
New York, NY 10012
Phone: 800-724-652-7842
www2.scholastic.com/browse/home.jsp

The Cat in the Hat by Dr. Seuss is available from Random House. The cost is $8.99.

Random House
1745 Broadway
New York, NY 10019
Phone: 212-782-9000
www.randomhouse.com/

Detective LaRue: Letters from the Investigation by Mark Teague is available from Scholastic. The cost is $15.95.

Scholastic Inc.
557 Broadway
New York, NY 10012
Phone: 800-724-652-7842
www2.scholastic.com/browse/home.jsp

The Drinking Gourd by F. N. Monjo is available from HarperCollins. The cost is $3.99.

HarperCollins
10 East 53rd Street
New York, NY 10022
Phone: 212-207-7000
www.harpercollins.com/

Encyclopedia Brown Gets His Man by Donald J. Sobel is available from Penguin Group. The cost is $4.99.

Penguin Group
375 Hudson Street
New York, NY 10014
Phone: 800-847-5515
http://us.penguingroup.com/

Fables by Arnold Lobel is available from HarperCollins. The cost is $6.99.

HarperCollins
10 East 53rd Street
New York, NY 10022
Phone: 212-207-7000
www.harpercollins.com/

The Gum Chewing Rattler by Joe Hayes is available from Cinco Puntos Press. The cost is $17.95.

Cinco Puntos Press
701 Texas
El Paso, Texas 79901
Phone: 800-566-9072
www.cincopuntos.com/index.sstg

Hedgie Blasts Off! by Jan Brett is available from Penguin Group. The cost is $16.99.

Penguin Group
375 Hudson Street
New York, NY 10014
Phone: 800-847-5515
http://us.penguingroup.com/

Imogene's Antlers by David Small is available from Random House. The cost is $8.99.

Random House
1745 Broadway
New York, NY 1001
Phone: 212-782-9000
www.randomhouse.com/

John, Paul, George, and Ben by Lane Smith is available from Amazon. The cost is $16.99.

Amazon
www.amazon.com

Johnny Appleseed by Steven Kellog is available from Scholastic. The cost is $5.95.

Scholastic Inc.
557 Broadwa
New York, NY 10012
Phone: 800-724-652-7842
www2.scholastic.com/browse/home.jsp

Joyful Noise: Poems for Two Voices by Paul Fleischman is available from HarperCollins. The cost is $5.99.

HarperCollins
10 East 53rd Street
New York, NY 10022
Phone: 212-207-7000
www.harpercollins.com/

June 29, 1999 by David Wiesner is available from Clarion Books, an imprint of HoughtonMifflin. The cost is $16.00.

> Houghton Mifflin Company
> Trade Customer Service
> 181 Ballardvale Street
> P.O. Box 7050
> Wilmington, MA 01887
> Phone: 800-225-3362
> *www.houghtonmifflinbooks.com*

Junie B., First Grader (at last!) by Barbara Park is available from Random House. The cost is $4.99.

> Random House
> 1745 Broadway
> New York, NY 10019
> Phone: 212-782-9000
> *www.randomhouse.com*

Kickoff by Tiki Barber is available from Simon & Schuster. The cost is $15.99.

> Simon & Schuster
> 1230 Avenue of the Americas, 11th Fl.
> New York, NY 10020
> Phone: 212-698-7000
> *www.simonsays.com*

Knots in My Yo-Yo String by Jerry Spinelli is available from Random House. The cost is $10.95.

> Random House
> 1745 Broadway
> New York, NY 10019
> Phone: 212-782-9000
> *www.randomhouse.com*

The Legend of the Bluebonnet by Tomie DePaola is available from Penguin Group. The cost is $16.99.

> Penguin Group
> 375 Hudson Street
> New York, NY 10014
> Phone: 800-847-5515
> *http://us.penguingroup.com/*

The Legend of the Indian Paintbrush by Tomie DePaola is available from Penguin Group. The cost is $16.99.

> Penguin Group
> 375 Hudson Street
> New York, NY 10014

> Phone: 800-847-5515
> *http://us.penguingroup.com/*

Little Red Riding Hood by Trina Schart Hyman is available from Holiday House. The cost is $17.95.

> Holiday House
> 425 Madison Avenue
> New York, NY 10017
> Fax: 212-421-6134
> *www.holidayhouse.com/index.php*

Martin's Big Words: the Life of Martin Luther King, Jr. by Doreen Rappaport is available from Amazon. The cost is $6.99.

> Amazon
> *www.amazon.com*

Mufaro's Beautiful Daughters by John Steptoe is available from HarperCollins. The cost is $16.99.

> HarperCollins
> 10 East 53rd Street
> New York, NY 10022
> Phone: 212-207-7000
> *www.harpercollins.com/*

My Great-Aunt Arizona by Gloria Houston is available from HarperCollins. The cost is $6.99.

> HarperCollins
> 10 East 53rd Street
> New York, NY 10022
> Phone: 212-207-7000
> *www.harpercollins.com*

Once a Mouse by Marcia Brown is available from Simon & Schuster. The cost is $17.99.

> Simon & Schuster
> 1230 Avenue of the Americas, 11th Fl.
> New York, NY 10020
> Phone: 212-698-7000
> *www.simonsays.com*

Pink and Say by Patricia Polacco is available from Penguin Group. The cost is $16.99.

> Penguin Group
> 375 Hudson Street
> New York, NY 1001
> Phone: 800-847-5515
> *http://us.penguingroup.com/*

Rapunzel by Paul O. Zelinsky is available from Penguin Group. The cost is $17.99.

> Penguin Group
> 375 Hudson Street
> New York, NY 10014
> Phone: 800-847-5515
> *http://us.penguingroup.com/*

Ricky Ricotta's Giant Robot by Dav Pilkey is available from Scholastic. The cost is $3.99.

> Scholastic Inc.
> 557 Broadway
> New York, NY 10012
> Phone: 800-724-652-7842
> *www2.scholastic.com/browse/home.jsp*

Saint George and the Dragon by Margaret Hodges is available from Little, Brown and Young, part of Hachette Book Group. The cost is $17.99.

> Hachette Book Group
> Center Plaza
> Boston, MA 02108
> Phone: 800-759-0190
> *www.hachettebookgroupusa.com/index.aspx*

Snowflake Bentley by Jacqueline Briggs Martin available from HoughtonMifflin. The cost is $16.00.

> Houghton Mifflin Company
> Trade Customer Service
> 181 Ballardvale Street
> P.O. Box 7050
> Wilmington, MA 01887
> Phone: 800-225-3362
> *www.houghtonmifflinbooks.com*

The Tortoise and the Hare by Janet Stevens is available from Holiday House. The cost is $17.95.

> Holiday House
> 425 Madison Avenue
> New York, NY 10017
> Fax: 212-421-6134
> *www.holidayhouse.com/index.php*

The Wall: My Life Growing Up Behind the Red

Curtain by Peter Sis is available from Farrar, Straus, and Giroux, an imprint of Macmillan. The cost is $18.00.

> Farrar, Straus & Giroux
> 18 West 18th St
> New York, NY 10011
> Phone: 212-741-6900
> *http://us.macmillan.com/FSG.aspx*

When Sophie Gets Angry—Really, Really Angry by Molly Bang is available from Scholastic. The cost is $12.76.

> Scholastic Inc.
> 557 Broadway
> New York, NY 10012
> Phone: 800-724-652-7842
> *www2.scholastic.com/browse/home.jsp*

Where the Sidewalk Ends by Shel Silverstein is available from HarperCollins. The cost is $18.99.

> HarperCollins
> 10 East 53rd Street
> New York, NY 10022
> Phone: 212-207-7000
> *www.harpercollins.com*

Where the Wild Things Are by Maurice Sendak is available from HarperCollins. The cost is $8.95.

> HarperCollins
> 10 East 53rd Street
> New York, NY 10022
> Phone: 212-207-7000
> *www.harpercollins.com*

You Read to Me, I'll Read to You series by Mary Ann Hoberman is available from Little, Brown and Young, part of Hachette Book Group. The cost is $16.99.

> Hachette Book Group
> Center Plaza
> Boston, MA 02108
> Phone: 800-759-0190
> *www.hachettebookgroupusa.com/index.aspx*

Chapter 10

New York Times Bestseller List
www.nytimes.com/pages/books/bestseller/

Reading Rainbow
http://pbskids.org/readingrainbow/

Spaghetti Book Club
www.spaghettibookclub.org/

Other

The Rubistar website was used in the creation of rubrics for these units.

Rubistar
http://rubistar.4teachers.org/index.php